Chinggis Khan
World Conqueror

Image of Chinggis Khan on a late twentieth-century Mongolian banknote (the tugrit), based on official Yuan (Chinese) portrait © Ruth Dunnell/Ruth W. Dunnell.

Ruth W. Dunnell
Kenyon College

Chinggis Khan
World Conqueror

THE LIBRARY OF WORLD BIOGRAPHY

Edited by Peter N. Stearns

Longman
Boston   Columbus   Indianapolis   New York   San Francisco   Upper Saddle River
Amsterdam   Cape Town   Dubai   London   Madrid   Milan   Munich   Paris   Montreal   Toronto
Delhi   Mexico City   Sao Paulo   Sydney   Hong Kong   Seoul   Singapore   Taipei   Tokyo

Editorial Director: Leah Jewell
Acquisitions Editor: Charles Cavaliere
Editorial Assistant: Lauren Aylward
Director of Marketing: Brandy Dawson
Project Manager: Renata Butera
Operations Specialist: Renata Butera
Creative Art Director: Jayne Conte
Cover Designer: Bruce Kenselaar
Manager, Cover Visual Research & Permissions: Karen Sanatar
Cover Image Credit: (C) The Bridgeman Art Library
Manager, Rights and Permissions: Zina Arabia
Manager, Visual Research: Beth Brenzel
Cover Art: Cover illustration: "Chingiz Khan in battle," Fourteenth century Persian
   miniature from Ahmad Tabrizi's *Shahanshahnama* (a collection of epic poems),
   British Library Or. 2780, f.49v.
Full-Service Project Management/Composition: Joseph Malcolm/GGS Higher Education Resources
Printer/Binder: Courier-Stoughton
Image Permission Coordinator: Craig A. Jones
Cover Printer: Demand Production Center
Text Font: 10/12 Sabon

Library of Congress Cataloging-in-Publication Data
 Dunnell, Ruth W.,
   Chinggis Khan: world conqueror / Ruth W. Dunnell.—1st ed.
   p. cm.—(Library of world biography series)
 Includes bibliographical references and index.
 ISBN-13: 978-0-321-27633-9
 ISBN-10: 0-321-27633-7
   1. Genghis Khan, 1162-1227.   2. Mongols—Kings and rulers—Biography.
3. Mongols—History—To 1500.   4. Mongolia—History.   5. Conquerors—Eurasia—Biography.
I. Title.
 DS22.D84 2010
 950'.21092—dc22

                                                              2009030248

Longman
is an imprint of

www.pearsonhighered.com

10 9 8 7 6 5 4 3 2 1

ISBN-13: 978-0-321-27633-9
ISBN-10:   0-321-27633-7

For Lotte Louise

Contents

Editor's Preface

Biography is history seen through the prism of a person.

—Louis Fischer

It is often challenging to identify the roles and experiences of individuals in world history. Larger forces predominate, yet biography provides important access to world history. It shows how individuals helped shape the society around them. Biography also offers concrete illustrations of larger patterns in political and intellectual life, family life, and the economy.

The Longman Library of World Biography series seeks to capture the individuality and drama that mark human character. It deals with individuals operating in one of the main periods of world history, while also reflecting issues in the particular society around them. Here, the individual illustrates larger themes of time and place. The interplay between the personal and general is always the key to using biography in history, and world history is no exception. Always, too, there is a question of personal agency: How much do individuals, even the great ones, shape their own lives and environment, and how much are they shaped by the world around them?

PETER N. STEARNS

Author's Preface

Undertaking a new biography of a world figure about whom so many have written so much is a daunting task. Yet many of us who teach the Mongol Empire, either in passing or in depth, to undergraduate students have felt the absence of a concise, historically sensitive, unsensationalizing, and affordable biography, one that tells a gripping tale yet also helps students to think through the larger implications of an individual life and how the stories told about that individual and community have come down to us. In the case of someone like Chinggis Khan, there are many ways that such a book could be written; this is only one. It reflects my life-long interest in the history of cultural and other kinds of interactions between the Chinese world and the world of the peoples who lived in the vast expanses between China and Europe. It also reflects my belief that the history of those peoples, Eurasian steppe nomads and Mongols among them, operated according to principles that we are only beginning to understand, and that the more we try to uncover their dynamics, the better we will understand our own histories.

This work owes large debts to the many talented scholars whose research has opened up interpretative breakthroughs and furnished the depth of detail that now enriches the study of the Mongols and their empire. It was not possible to include all of them in this biography. I am likewise grateful to the numerous readers for Longmans who provided extensive and extremely helpful comments on the manuscript in progress: David Blaylock, Eastern Kentucky University; Michael Brose, University of Wyoming; Andrew F. Clark, University of North Carolina, Wilimington; Marcus Cox, The Citadel; Michael Farmer, Brigham Young University; James Farr, Purdue University; Dean T. Ferguson, Texas A&M University, Kingsville; Ari Levine, University of Georgia; Timothy May, North Georgia College and State University; John A. Nichols, Slippery Rock University; David Price, Santa Fe College; David Roxburgh, Harvard University. Even where I disagreed with some observation, it forced me to rethink my choices in ways that were always fruitful.

As for my patient daughter, I only hope that one day she will want to read the book that prompted her mother to whisk her off to Mongolia one summer when she was almost nine.

Genealogical and Reign Chart of the Golden Lineage of Chinggis Khan

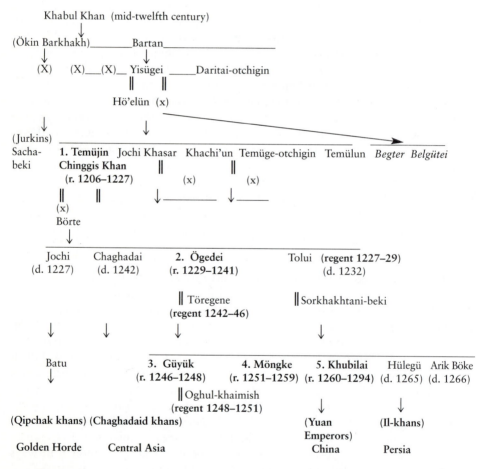

Genealogical and Reign Chart of the Golden Lineage of Chinggis Khan

*(Names in **bold** reigned as great khan; ‖ indicates marital connection; the khans all died in the year their reigns ended.)*

Persons Mentioned
in the Text

Mongol names, including names of persons adopted into Chinggis's family, appear in boldface.

'Ala al-Din Muhammad II: r. 1200–1220; sultan or shah of Khwarazm, a central Asian state south of the Aral Sea, died fleeing from Mongols early in 1221

Alakhush Digit Khuri: early thirteenth-century chief of the Önggüts, a Turkic people along the northern frontier of China, in Chinese sources also called "White Tatars" to distinguish them from the Mongols (Black Tatars). *Digit khuri* means "hereditary chieftain"; Alakhush was an early supporter of Chinggis Khan

Alan Gho'a: mythical ancestress of the Mongols in the *Secret History*

Altan: older cousin of Chinggis Khan; one of the senior members of the Kiyat Borjigin lineage who sponsored Temüjin's first election as khan

Ambaghai: cousin and successor of Khabul Khan, first Mongol chieftain who tried in the early twelfth century to unify the tribes against the Jin

Arik Böke: younger son of Tolui, unsuccessful rival of older brother Khubilai.

Arslan Khan: chief of the Qarluq Turks in the steppes south of Lake Balkhash, in central Asia; submitted to Chinggis Khan in 1211

Asan: see Hasan Hajji

Asha Gambu: anti-Mongol minister at the Tangut Xia court in the early thirteenth century

'Ata Malik Juvaini (1226–1283): Persian court historian and official under the Mongol rulers of Iran, author of *History of the World Conqueror*, an early biography of Chinggis Khan

Barchuk Art Tegin: Uighur ruler (*iduqut*) in the early thirteenth century; another early supporter of Chinggis Khan

Begter: stepbrother killed by Temüjin and Khasar

Belgütei: the other stepbrother of Chinggis Khan; renowned for his physical strength

Bo'orchu: Temüjin's youthful companion and first *nökör* who helped him to rescue a bunch of stolen horses; later a chief commander (of the Right Wing) in the Mongol army

Börte: principal wife of Chinggis Khan; only her sons were eligible to succeed the Khan

Büri Bökö: renowned Jurkin wrestler who paid with his life for humiliating Chinggis's stepbrother Belgütei in the early 1190s

Buyirukh khan: Naiman leader, sharing power with brother Tayang khan in final confrontation with Chinggis Khan

Chaghadai: second son of Temüjin and Börte; ancestor of the central Asian Chaghadaid khans

Changchun: 1148–1227; Daoist master invited from north China to Chinggis Khan's camp in central Asia (lay name Qiu Chuji)

Daritai-otchigin: an uncle of Temüjin; younger brother of Yisügei

Dei Sechen: Onggirat chieftain and father of Börte, principal wife of Chinggis Khan

Gürbesü Khatun: wife (stepmother) of Naiman ruler Tayang khan, foe of Chinggis

Hasan Hajji: Muslim merchant plying the trade routes between northern China and central Asia; assisted Chinggis Khan at Baljuna in 1203 and later during the central Asian campaigns

Hö'elün: mother of Chinggis Khan; belonged to the Onggirat tribe

Hülegü: 1217–1265; son of Tolui (Chinggis's youngest son) and Sorkhakhtani-beki; and brother of Mönkge, Khubilai, and Arik Böke; founder of the Il-khanid dynasty in Persia, ruling there ca. 1256–1265

Jafar: Khwarazmian merchant who took Baljuna oath with Chinggis; played key role in the conquest of Jin capital at Zhongdu and in negotiations with 'Ala al-Din Muhammad

Jakha Gambu: Ong-khan's younger brother, whose daughters became wives of Chinggis Khan's eldest son Jochi and youngest son Tolui

Jalal al-Din: charismatic son of Muhammad, the Khwarazm-shah; eluded Mongol capture for many years; slain in the mountains by Kurds in 1231

Jamukha: orphan of the Mongol Jadaran clan; Temüjin's childhood blood brother and rival to khanship over the Mongols and other tribes, died ca. 1205; portrayed as a sly, spiteful, untrustworthy person in later Mongol sources

Jebe: one of the "four hounds" (fierce warriors) of Chinggis Khan, recruited from among the defeated Tayichi'ut in 1201; with Sübetei raced around southwest Asia and up through Caucasus chasing the son of the Khwarazm-shah and defeating various peoples in battle before galloping back to Mongolia

Jelme: early adherent of Chinggis Khan, one of his "four hounds"

Jochi: d. 1227; eldest son of Temüjin and Börte, ancestor of the Golden Horde khans (Jochids)

John of Plano Carpini: fat Franciscan priest, who at age 65 traveled at behest of Pope Innocent IV in 1245 to the Mongol court at Kharakhorum, arriving in time to witness Güyük's enthronement as khan, and returning via southern Russia in 1247

Khabul Khan: mid-twelfth century Mongol khan, unsuccessful in uniting the Mongols

Khachi'un: second younger brother of Chinggis Khan

Khasar: also Jochi Khasar; younger brother and sometimes rival of Chinggis Khan

Khubilai: second son of Tolui (Chinggis's youngest son) and Sorkhakhtani-beki, fifth ruler of the Mongol empire and founder of Yuan dynasty in China

Khudu: son of Merkit ruler Toghto'a beki who escaped into central Asia and joined up there with Küchlüg; killed by Mongols ca. 1216

Khulan-khatun: a defeated Merkit princess and prominent wife of Chinggis Khan

Khutula: mid-twelfth century Mongol khan, son of Kabul Khan, ancestor of Chinggis; killed while battling the Tatars

Khwarazm-shah Muhammad: see 'Ala al-Din Muhammad

Kuchar: older cousin of Chinggis Khan; senior member of the Kiyat Borjigin lineage who sponsored Temüjin's first election as khan

Küchlüg: son and heir of Naiman ruler Tayang khan; escaped to the Qara Khitai realm in central Asia and usurped its throne, died ca. 1218 at Mongol hands; *also Güchülük*

Mahmud Yalavic: Khwarazmian merchant; a member of Chinggis Khan's delegation to Samarqand in 1218; later a prominent Mongol administrator in Turkestan; *also Mahmud Yalavach*

Marco Polo: son of a Venetian merchant family who traveled with uncles to Italian markets in southwest Asia, then overland to Mongol-ruled China in the early 1270s, returning to Venice ca. 1295. The later account of his travels, written down by a prison-mate during a brief incarceration, has inspired curiosity, passion, and skepticism among generations of readers

Möngke: r. 1251–1259; eldest son of Tolui (Chinggis's youngest son) and Sorkhakhtani-beki, fourth ruler of the Mongol empire

Mönglik: son of Yisügei's old retainer; possibly Hö'elün's husband after Yisügei's death; father of seven sons, among whom Teb Tenggri gave Temüjin the name "Chinggis"; *also "Father Mönglik"*

Mukhali: d. 1223; a Jalayir, or subject tribesman, of the Jurkin clan and later a slave in Temüjin's camp; celebrated warrior; head of the Mongol army's Left Wing

Ögedei: third son of Temüjin and Börte; successor to Chinggis (r. 1229–1241 as Great Khan)

Ong-khan: title of Toghril, khan of the Kereyits (see under Toghril)

Prester John: legendary Christian king in western Christian folklore, located variously in eastern Africa or east Asia, identified either with the Qara Khitai founder (who was a Buddhist) or with Ong-khan (who was a Christian); rumors figured him coming to help liberate the Holy Land from Muslim occupation

Rashid al-Din: 1247–1318; official and historian under the Mongol Il-khans of Persia

Sacha-beki: older cousin of Chinggis Khan; senior member of the Kiyat Borjigin lineage who sponsored Temüjin's first election as khan

Senggüm: Ilkha Senggüm, son and heir of Kereyit chief Ong-khan

Shigi-khutukhu: d. 1260; Tatar foundling adopted into Chinggis's family; first judge or *jarguchi* of the Mongol Empire

Sorkhakhtani-beki: daughter of Ong-khan's younger brother, Jakha-gambu; married to Tolui, Chinggis's youngest son; mother of four khans: Möngke (r. 1251–1259), Khubilai (r. 1260–1294), Hülegü (first Il-khan of Persia, ca. 1256–1265), and Arik Böke (d. 1266, rival of Khubilai)

Sorkhan Shira: Tayichi'ut tribal subordinate who assisted a young Temüjin to escape captivity

Sübetei: d. 1248; one of the "four hounds" of Chinggis's and most famous general, campaigned in north China, southwest Asia, Russia, and eastern Europe; belonged to the Uriyangkhai clan; joined Chinggis in ca. 1203 at Baljuna

Tamerlane: Timur (Persian form of Temür), ca. 1336–1405; central Asian conqueror of Turko-Mongol descent (not a Chinggisid); founder of Timurid dynasty

Tarkhutai: Tayichi'ud chieftain; cousin of Yisügei

Tata-tonga: literate Uighur serving Naiman court, captured in campaign of 1204; introduced bureaucracy to emerging Mongol government

Tayang khan: Naiman leader, sharing power with brother Buyirukh khan, in final confrontation with Chinggis Khan to unite the Mongol tribes

Teb Tenggeri: middle son of Father Mönglik; powerful shaman who gave Temüjin the epithet "Chinggis" (The Fierce); suffered execution in a wrestling match after challenging the khan's authority

Temüge-otchigin: youngest brother of Chinggis Khan

Temüjin: 1162–1227; personal name of Chinggis Khan, after the Tatar chief his father had killed right before his first son's birth

Temülün: youngest full sibling and sister of Chinggis Khan

Terken-khatun: mother of Khwarazm-shah Muhammad, a Qangli Turk princess

Toghril: aging khan of the Kereyit federation, received the title Ong (*wang*, "prince") from Jin in 1190s for his military service against the Tatars; sworn brother of Chinggis Khan's father

Toghto'a-beki: enemy Merkit chief who eluded Chinggis until 1208

Tolui: youngest son of Temüjin and Börte; ancestor of the Il-khans and Yuan emperors (Toluids)

Töregene: main wife of Great Khan Ögedei (d. 1241); reigned as regent during 1242–1246

Yelu Ahai: an early Khitan defector to Chinggis Khan

Yelü Chucai: literate Khitan subject of Jin recruited by the Mongols after their seizure of the Jin capital in 1214; spent several years in central Asia and kept a diary of his travels; prominent advisor to Mongol rulers in north China

Yisügei: father of Chinggis Khan

Chronology: The Rise of the Mongol Empire

Key events in the life of Chinggis Khan, and reign dates of later Great Khans, appear in boldface; for comparative purposes, a few contemporary events taking place elsewhere appear in italics.

900s	Mongols migrate out of Manchuria into northeast Mongolia
907	Khitans establish Liao Empire in north Asia, along Chinese frontier
960	Chinese Song dynasty founded, capital at Kaifeng in north China
1038	Tanguts found Xia dynasty, in northwest China; *Xia produced earliest extant texts printed with moveable type, invented in China in eleventh century*
1115	Jurchens found Jin dynasty in Manchuria
1125–1127	Jurchens capture last Liao emperor, take over north China from Song
1127	(Southern) Song re-established at Hangzhou, in the Yangzi River valley
ca. 1130	Yelu Dashi reestablishes a Khitan state in central Asia (Qara Khitai)
1140s	Mongol attacks on Jin gain them favorable treaty terms
1150s–1160s	Tatars turn over Mongol khan to Jurchen, ending Mongol efforts to unify; *Frankish Crusaders invade Egypt*
ca. 1162	**birth of Temüjin, future Chinggis Khan**
ca. 1172	**death of Yisügei, Temüjin's father**
ca. 1182	**alliance with Ong-khan and joint campaign to rescue Börte**
1185–1189	**Temüjin elected khan by his relatives;** *Saladin, founder of Ayyubid dynasty, takes Jerusalem 1187; King Richard I crowned in London, 1189; Minamoto Yoritomo established first bakufu (shogunal government) at Kamakura, Japan*
1196	**Tatar campaign**
1199	Mongol–Kereyit battle with Naimans; *Richard I killed in France*
1200	Mongol–Kereyit attack on Tayichi'uts; *'Ala al-Din Muhammad becomes Khwarazm-shah*
1201	Jamukha made khan by foes of Temüjin, battle of Köyiten
1203	**Mongols break with Kereyits; defeat Ong-khan; Temüjin becomes Kereyit khan**
1204	Mongols defeat Naimans; Naiman and Merkit princes flee; *Fourth Crusade sacks Constantinople*
ca. 1205	death of Jamukha; first raid on Tangut Xia territory

1206–1227	reign of Temüjin as Chinggis Khan
1206	Temüjin proclaimed khan with new name Chinggis; *Dresden founded*
1209	Uighur ruler tenders allegiance; Tangut ruler pledges allegiance to Chinggis after Mongols besiege capital
1210	Chinggis severs tributary relations with Jin court
1211	Mongol armies advance into north China
1215	Zhongdu falls to Mongols, north China in chaos; birth of Khubilai, future Great Khan (r. 1260–1294); *adoption of Magna Carta in England*
1217	Chinggis sends diplomatic mission to Khwarazm-shah
1218–1219	Mongol trade delegation to Khwarazm-shah murdered at Otrar; Muhammad kills Mongol envoys; death of Naiman pretender Küchlüg
1219	Mongol armies advance into central Asia, reach Otrar in fall
1220	Otrar reduced in late winter, Bukhara in February, Samarqand in March; Chinggis sends Jebe and Sübetei to capture Muhammad and son, and summers in Hindu Kush
1221	Muhammad dies; Chinggis attacks Khurasan and Iraq; siege of Urganch; Chinggis receives news of trouble in north China and withdraws; Jebe and Sübetei campaign around Caspian, Caucasus, and Black sea steppes; *Crusaders defeated in Egypt at battle of Mansurah*
1222–1223	Chinggis and Daoist sage Changchun meet in Hindu Kush and Samarqand; Jebe and Sübetei defeat Russians at Khalka River; *Chartres Cathedral completed*
1224–1225	Chinggis back at camp on Irtysh River, Mongolia, by spring 1225
1226	Mongols campaign against Tangut Xia; *death of Francis of Assisi*
1227	Jochi dead by 1227; Chinggis Khan dies (age 66 roughly) in August at the end of Xia campaign; youngest son Tolui becomes regent
1229–1241	**reign of Ögedei as Great Khan**
1234	Jin empire reduced; Mongols take over north China
1235	construction begins on capital at Kharakhorum, central Mongolia
1237–1242	Batu campaigns in Russia and eastern Europe (Poland and Hungary, 1241)
1245–1247	John of Plano Carpini travels to Mongolia and Kharakhorum
1246–1248	**reign of Güyüg as Great Khan**
1251–1259	**reign of Mönke as Great Khan**
1252–1253	'Ata Malik Juvaini visits Kharakhorum
1253–1255	William of Rubruck travels to Mongolia and Kharakhorum
1258	Hülegü conquers Bagdad, ends 'Abbasid Caliphate; submission of Korea to Khubilai
1260–1294	**reign of Khubilai as Great Khan**
1271	Khubilai founds Yuan dynasty in north China, capital at Dadu (Beijing)
1274 and 1281	unsuccessful Mongol invasions of Japan
1271–1295	Marco Polo's travels to Asia and China
1275–1279	Khubilai completes conquest of south China (Song dynasty)

List of Maps
and Illustrations

Introduction

In recent decades, the image of the medieval conquering Mongols has been significantly modified, showing yet again how the present shapes the past. The shift in perception rests on impressive advances in scholarship on the Mongol Empire and larger economic and political changes in the world. Among other things, the country Mongolia has been transformed from a communist cold war client of Russia and China into a fledgling democracy and tourist destination.

From the perspective of an early twenty-first century scholar, the medieval Mongols appear as early adepts of globalization, linking the remote ends of the Eurasian continent through diplomatic, military, commercial, microbial, and cultural exchanges. Sam Adshead has stated that world history as such began with the Mongolian "explosion" of Chinggis Khan, which "broke down barriers . . . ended isolation . . . and produced the first of the permanent world institutions: the basic information circuit." This idea extends the meaning of the phrase invented earlier by scholars, *Pax Mongolica* (Mongol Peace), which refers to the Mongol opening up and patrolling of Eurasian trade routes. Adshead reminds us that it was the work of the two successors of Chinggis which made this event a global one. Although the Mongols, as a land-based empire, are most commonly associated with securing the routes across Eurasia, encouraging transcontinental travel, they also encouraged maritime trade and developed a considerable navy from 1260s onward, in the course of conquering southern China. Their famous failure to take Japan by naval assault has perhaps obscured the important contributions they made to east Asian sea power, mainly through the mobilization of skilled Chinese, Korean, and Muslim sailors, shipbuilders, and engineers. As a war machine, the navy of Mongol-ruled China was peerless.

The Mongol Empire now appears as the Asian prompt to the Columbian exchange that followed its fourteenth-century fragmentation by barely a hundred years. Christopher Columbus had read the *Travels* of Marco Polo, who was only the most famous visitor to the court of the Great Khan Khubilai (Chinggis Khan's grandson). Columbus kept a copy of Polo's book on board when he sailed off to find not the New World, but a northern sea route to China, whose fabled wealth had been made more accessible by the Mongol Empire. But equally important, and more immediate, were the institutional innovations set in motion by Chinggis Khan and expanded upon by his sons and successors. In exploring the premodern world trading system of ca. 1250–1350, Janet Abu-Lughod has stressed the function of *Pax Mongolica* as facilitating Eurasian exchange, noting the inherent instabilities caused by "political and demographic fluctuations" and the "parasitic nature" of Mongols who "neither traded nor produced." Yet as Thomas Allsen's more recent researches have painstakingly demonstrated, the Mongols were not passive participants who merely *facilitated* historical processes: They *created* demands for new commodities and reshaped existing networks or built new structures for the production and circulation of these commodities as well as the people who made them. Their governing priorities and practices shaped the Muscovite state in Russia, the late imperial states in China and Korea, and the many successor regimes in central and southwest Asia. The thirteenth-century Mongol conquests reunified China, which had been divided since the early tenth century into regional states, and China remained unified thereafter.

This book's interpretation of Chinggis Khan, who is more familiar under the spelling Genghis Khan (a European misreading of a Persian form of the name), is deeply indebted to the perennial fascination with the Mongols, which has inspired scholars, authors of popular accounts, scientists, archaeologists, and adepts of electronic and entertainment media. It aims to present as clear an account as possible of who Chinggis Khan was, where he came from, why and how he pursued his career as a "world conqueror," and what it meant to the world then and later. This book tries to do so in a way that allows the reader to understand how a historian makes sense of the past on its own terms, as well as in ways that make sense to us today. It is not an exhaustive or scholarly account of the Mongol Empire; curious students will find many more specialized volumes in the list of references at the back of this book.

In these pages, readers should gain insight into how the Mongols saw and experienced the world, and the logic of their actions in it. Although we cannot answer every question that might arise, we should assume that the Mongols under Chinggis Khan and his successors constructed their empire according to terms that made sense to them, terms about which we can make reasonable judgments based on the vast body of sources that we have access to still. We will find some of these terms internally inconsistent or incompatible with our own values; we may find others to be eminently sensible or even remarkable in their adaptation to new challenges. As with every historical phenomenon, complexity and ambiguity attend any reconstruction of the past for an audience of the writer's own time. In presenting and interpreting these complexities and ambiguities, the author hopes that the reader will enjoy puzzling them out.

So momentous an event as the Mongol conquests involved many people. To help readers keep track of key people, places, and the sequence of events, an annotated cast of all figures mentioned in the text appears before the first chapter, along with a chronology of key events. A genealogical and reign chart appears after the preface, and four maps are distributed throughout the text (see the list, following the Table of Contents, for their location). A glossary of terms appears after the last chapter, supplemented by a general index. Navigating the thickets of medieval Mongol and Eurasian nomenclature and relationships is actually less arduous than the overland journey from Europe to Kharakhorum (the imperial Mongol capital), and readers may take comfort in knowing that even experts trip over names and dates.

Some discussion of the sources for Mongol history is imperative. In the case of the Mongol Empire, no single author can master all of the written sources (quite apart from the visual and archeological records), in part because they exist in many different and quite difficult languages: Chinese (in which Korean records were kept as well as Chinese), Persian, Mongolian, Arabic, Turkish, Russian, Armenian, Georgian, Latin, Japanese, and others—testimony to the numbers of people touched by this singular episode. Even though many important medieval texts are now available in English translation, no serious scholar of the Mongol Empire can dispense with language study. But being able to read a text does not guarantee understanding it, given the cultural distance between then and now, so imagination and an interest in comparative history play a role too.

Another kind of understanding involves the recognition that many of our best sources, including the ones used here, were written by people about whom we sometimes know nothing or very little, who had a distinct political interest or cultural predisposition in presenting the events narrated by them in a particular fashion. Given the deadly politics of Mongol succession disputes, and the fact that many of our authors served at the pleasure of Mongol overlords, one must read the sources carefully, against one another. People at a safe distance from the centers of Mongol power might write what they pleased, but that does not necessarily assure their greater objectivity or accuracy. Writers enjoying Mongol patronage typically could lay hands on more authoritative information than those who relied on second- and third-hand reports.

The Persian and Chinese materials stand above all others in quantity and quality, mostly because Iran and China had long traditions of literate bureaucracies and elites who valued writing things down. Iran and China were the two richest regions in the empire and thus generated a lot of documents. Persian and Chinese bureaucrats also strove to normalize what must have often seemed to them an irregular operation at best. They shared in common the fact that the rulers of Yuan China and Il-khanate Persia descended from two allied brothers, Hülegü and Khubilai, both offspring of Chinggis Khan's youngest son Tolui; therefore, in various ways Toluid sources represent points of view favorable to the branch of Chinggis Khan's family that emerged victorious in the succession battle of 1260–1264. As the saying goes, the winners write the history.

This account draws upon translations of the chronicles of two major Persian court historians of the thirteenth and early fourteenth centuries, who participated in the events recorded by them or had direct access to Mongolian sources of information close to the center of action. 'Ata Malik Juvaini (1226–1283), scion of a distinguished family and like his father a Mongol official in northeastern Iran, visited the Mongol imperial capital at Kharakhorum in 1252–1253 and began thereupon to write a *History of the World Conqueror*. After the Mongol conquest of the Caliph of Baghdad and his realm in 1258, Juvaini was appointed as governor of the area. His history thus provides an exceptionally vivid window onto the imperial Mongols. He died in 1283, and his family perished soon after in a succession struggle in Mongol Iran that may have sent Juvaini to his death as well.

Juvaini's younger peer, Rashid al-Din (1247–1318), served as a trusted minister to several Mongol rulers of Iran, and supervised the compilation of what is widely regarded as the first universal history, *Compendium of Chronicles*, by far the single most informative source for the Mongol Empire overall. Rashid al-Din was born as the son of a Jewish physician in central Iran, converted to Islam in the course of his career serving the Mongol court in Iran, and sponsored many charitable foundations. Involvement in court intrigue led to his execution in 1318, but his many surviving written works testify to his vast cultural legacy. For his history, Rashid drew upon the work of his predecessors, including Juvaini, and as a vizier or minister to a Mongol ruler, culled information from high-ranking Mongols and restricted Mongol documents that did not survive.

Mongol sources are scarce, but this is not so surprising after all when we recall that nomadic peoples developed extensive oral traditions but dispensed with the burden of carting around books and pens until their livelihoods came to require it. Fortunately a key Mongol source survived and is indispensable: the Mongols' own mid-thirteenth century version of their origins and the life of Chinggis Khan, a unique literary monument in prose and verse, half-epic half-chronicle, now known under the title of *The Secret History of the Mongols*. The mythologizing character of *The Secret History of the Mongols* has not only attracted much critical comment from historians, but also accounts for its appeal to readers. It is not known precisely when *The Secret History* was written down or who compiled it; the last paragraph informs us that the book was "completed at the time when the Great Assembly convened . . . in the Year of the Rat . . .," which could be 1228, 1240, or 1252, to name the most common hypotheses. The compiler must have been someone close to the events and people around whom the stories revolve. Later editors clearly added or deleted materials, or altered the text in other ways over the years. What it lacks in chronological accuracy and coverage, however, it makes up for in unique expression of Mongol cultural values. The *Secret History* is cited often in this book from the authoritative translation by Igor de Rachewiltz, who favors a 1228 date of composition, one year after Chinggis Khan's death. Rashid al-Din, the *Secret History*, and some Chinese records evidently all shared access to some key Mongol sources (no longer extant), given the overlap in their presentation of certain events.

Chinese official histories and unofficial writings of the Yuan era (1271–1368) supply much valuable information and are cited here as appropriate. Chinggis Khan was officially honored as the founder of the Yuan dynasty with the retrospective title of Yuan Taizu (Great Ancestor of the Yuan). His official Yuan portrait provided the basis of many subsequent images of the conqueror, including that now featured on the Mongolian currency (see Figure 10.1). Some of the well-known European travelers to the Mongol courts, such as the papal envoy John of Plano Carpini (a Franciscan friar), and merchant Marco Polo, also testify in these pages. The reader will find citations of these and other sources under References in the back, arranged by chapter, and followed by a general list of works consulted.

Spellings and names present vexing choices. This book follows a modified transcription for Mongolian and Turkic names and terms based on the system devised by Antoine Mostaert and used in *The Cambridge History of China, Vol. 6, Alien Regimes and Border States 907–1368*, and on Igor de Rachewiltz's usage in his translation of the *Secret History*. For the sake of simplicity and clarity, "kh" is preferred to "q" (khan instead of qan) in most instances. Central Asian names of Turkic origin are written with a "q," for example, the Qangli and Qipchak Turks, the Qara Khitai, and so on (see Glossary). This book indicates front vowels (e, ö, and ü) and back vowels (a, o, and u) in Mongolian personal names by using the umlaut over front vowels (as in Temüjin). The rule is simple: Whichever kind of vowel appears in the first syllable, the same kind must appear in subsequent syllables (the vowel "i" is neutral). Temüjin was the birth name of the man who later became Chinggis Khan and is used here in the first several chapters. For Chinese names and terms, this book employs the *pinyin* system of Romanization used worldwide and in China. In *pinyin* "q" is *not* pronounced like "kh" but like "ch" (as in Qin, "cheen").

Tatar, more familiar as Tartar, refers to an old and mighty Mongol-speaking tribe, which remained so prominent in the unified Mongolian federation that its name superseded that of its masters in the western reaches of the empire. Once they had absorbed the Tatar federation, the early Mongols might informally use the name to refer to themselves when speaking with people (such as the Chinese) accustomed to dealing with the Tatars. The Europeans assimilated the name to the Greek *tartarus*, or hell (also a deity in Greek mythology); European writers down to the twentieth century used the word *Tartar* to name Asian nomadic conquerors of various sorts, including the Manchus, the last foreign conquerors of China. The early twentieth-century Chinese revolutionary, Sun Yat-sen, when writing in English on one occasion referred to the Muslims living in China as "Tartars" and distinguished them from Mongols and Manchus.

Medieval Russians referred to their Mongol overlords as Tatars, and because the Tatar–Mongols in western Eurasia had become Turkicized by the fourteenth century, Tatar evolved into a new ethnonym (tribal name) for Turkic-speaking Muslim peoples of the former Russian Empire, the most prominent today being the Crimean Tatars.

The Persian form of "Mongol" has yielded another name, Moghal or Mughal. It became the name of the Delhi-based empire founded by the central Asian prince, Babur. Descended from Timur (Tamerlane), the late fourteenth-century conqueror of western central Asia who had both Mongol and Turk ancestry, Babur established a new home in north India in the early sixteenth century, after the last Timurid cities fell under new overlords.

Juvaini begins his *History of the World Conqueror* with an appropriately obsequious accolade to "the Commander of the Earth and Age, the source of the blessings of peace and security, the Khan of all Khans," in short, the reigning Great Khan Möngke (r. 1251–1229), with whom he had an audience in 1253. Friends suggested to him that he should write up the fruits of his journey to Kharakhorum, the Mongol steppe capital. In the service of rather different masters, the first chapter to this book lays out the basic themes that frame the interpretation presented here and its underlying assumptions in regard to the nomadic–sedentary relationship and nomadic state formation in Eurasia. It then sketches the geographical and historical setting of Eurasia on the eve of the Mongols' rise to power.

Chapter 2 analyzes the natural and social environment of the Mongols and their neighbors on the eve of Temüjin's birth. Subsequent chapters trace the key developments that shaped the future khan's destiny and that of his empire. The final chapter summarizes the themes in elaborating some of the principal legacies of Chinggis Khan's enterprise. Juvaini dwells in sometimes morbid and always vivid detail on the fate of his huge cast of characters, many contemporary to the author; his cast of thousands may dizzy the reader, but reminds us of what made the man at the center of his account.

Eurasian Nomads: Ecological, Geographical, and Historical Considerations

The greatest misfortune is for one to lose his father while he is young or his horse during a journey.

—MONGOL PROVERB

In the view of world historians, Eurasian peoples, nomads in particular, have played a crucial role in transregional communications and exchanges, certainly in the period 1000–1500 CE, or in some reckonings from as early as 1000 BCE to 1500 CE. Nomadic peoples and states, occupying ecological zones distinct from those of their sedentary neighbors, interacted with the latter in ways that fostered the spread of goods, technologies, religions, languages, and ideas. In this interpretation, nomadic peoples play a more positive role in world history than in earlier depictions, which tended to paint them in cruder colors as explosions of bloody barbarism from the depths of Asia into the civilized world, arising like the "primitive convulsions of nature," to quote the eighteenth-century historian Edward Gibbon, and leaving in their wake nothing but destruction, devastation, depopulation, oppression, and plague. Thus, in our global understanding, the historical identity of Eurasia's nomads has advanced from "natural catastrophes" to facilitators of intercultural or interregional exchange.

The Mongol conquests present a significant transitional point in Eurasia's part on the world historical stage, paving the way for the subsequent rise of the "West," the concomitant decline of transcontinental trade (superseded in historical significance, scholars deem, by maritime travel), and the incorporation of inner Eurasia into the great sedentary empires of Qing China, Romanov Russia, and Safavid Persia. Understanding how and why all of this happened requires deeper explanations, ones which may show that nomads did not simply "facilitate" exchange between sedentary peoples by transporting goods across inhospitable terrain, but indeed created and shaped the very terms of exchange in the course of building states, for example, to solve their own internal historical dilemmas. As this chapter introduces some of the elements at the core of these developments, it will undertake to define important terms used to denote them: *pastoralism, nomad, tribe,* and *Eurasia.*

Pastoral Nomads

The association of nomads with trade, raid, and conquest of settled peoples arises from their ecological adaptation to particular environments. Nomads, the kind of pastoralism they practiced, and the cultures that evolved with that practice varied greatly from one environment to the next. The focus of discussion here is primarily on the nomads of the steppes of inner Eurasia. Permanent mobility characterized these nomads and their practice of animal herding, and it is what distinguishes them from Texas cattle ranchers or Alpine shepherds. Whereas desert nomads, such as the Bedouins of North Africa, prized camels for transport and subsistence needs, steppe nomads cherished their horses and developed the arts of horseback riding and hunting in ways that made them feared and admired by their sedentary neighbors. Nomadic conquerors of any age, Huns, Turks, or Mongols, did not arrive on camelback, although camels performed valuable transport services for them.

Hunting, the earliest human adaptation to the inner Eurasian environment, remained an important subsistence strategy even after the domestication of sheep, goats, and cattle allowed for the cultivation of more dependable supplies of food. Domestication of the horse occurred later than that of these animals, probably on the rich grassland of the southern Russian steppe (the Pontic steppes), north of the Black Sea, around 4000 BCE. Pastoralism as a livelihood distinct from farming evolved later still; horse-riding pastoralists can be dated back only to around 1000 BCE. Pastoralists then combined the concentration of food resources (in mobile herds) with the concentration of defensive capability (in the organization of mounted warrior bands). Both defending herds and communal hunting honed physical and tactical skills that naturally fostered martial prowess and competition. Archaeological remains of the earliest horse-riding cultures on the steppes indicate that warfare concentrated resources and produced elites who were buried with their treasures.

Nomadic pastoralism (or pastoral nomadism) emerged when pastoralists left behind their settled cousins, packed their worldly goods on carts drawn by oxen or horses, and driving their herds of sheep and goats before them, struck out for new territories. They migrated in search of well-watered grasslands, pitching their mobile homes where conditions proved favorable and seeking sheltered camps to retreat to during the winter months, after the animals had fattened up on summer forage. Settling into regular seasonal migratory cycles, often moving vertically up into mountain pastures in summer and down into sheltered valleys in winter, nomads could maintain much larger herds than a sedentary farmer (see Figure 1.1 for a contemporary Mongolian rendition of their traditional lifestyle). Their animals provided milk and meat for nourishment (though they seldom slaughtered animals), wool and skins (of dead animals) from which to fashion clothing and tents, and sheep dung for fuel. Estimates are imprecise, but it seems that roughly a hundred animals constituted average herd size for a nomad family of four to five people; minimum subsistence evidently required a mixed herd of about fifty or sixty sheep, cattle, and horses, over half of which were the versatile and fertile sheep. Horses reigned as the source of prestige and object of cultural and cultic veneration.

Figure 1.1 Nomad Settlement, as reproduced from a Mongolian greeting card © Ruth Dunnell/Ruth W. Dunnell.

Nothing, however like "pure nomadism" ever existed, in which pastoral nomads pursued a self-sufficient livelihood, aloof from long-abandoned settled communities and proud of the ability to survive unaided in harsh lands. "Seminomadism" remained common during many periods in the history of Eurasia. For nomads, the mobile nature of their livelihood did not allow them to amass surpluses, and spring blizzards could wipe out a herd weakened by winter hunger. The only pure nomad, writers have quipped, was a poor nomad. From the beginning, nomads experimented with a range of survival strategies, adapting the mix of animals in their herds to the terrain, or where conditions allowed engaging in limited sowing of crops. Hunting supplemented food supplies. Pasture requirements for animals, and thus for human sustenance, make pastoral nomadism an extensive economy that cannot support more people or animals than the land available for grazing. This fact has limited the size and density of nomadic populations; surplus population must migrate elsewhere or turn to other forms of livelihood, such as peddlers, ironsmiths, caravan guards or mercenaries in someone's army, or as farmers.

Nomads commonly resorted to trade or raid to procure scarce or prized commodities such as grain, metal implements, and tea. Contacts with settled folks could be episodic and hostile unless some kind of regularized exchange was negotiated. But sedentary–nomadic relations were not uniformly hostile and spanned a continuum from symbiosis to warfare depending on the locale and circumstances, just as people's economic adaptations spanned a continuum from pastoral nomadism to sedentary farming. Symbiosis emerged between nomads and farmers on the Tibetan plateau, and between nomads and oases settlers in central Asia. As the eleventh-century central Asian writer Mahmud Kashgari commented, "There is no Turk without a Tadjik, there is no hat without a head," Turks and Tadjiks (Iranian-speaking inhabitants of central Asian oases states) representing nomads and sedentarists, respectively. Traditionally, nomads expressed a certain disdain for farmers, and settled peoples likewise looked down on and feared nomads; yet mutual dependence, both political and economic, evolved over centuries of Turkic migration into central Asia.

An example of negotiated exchange was the nomads' ability to exact tribute from settled communities in the form of payment in kind or regularized trading opportunities. Such arrangements did not require the presence of organized states on either side, although they did showcase the skills of nomadic chieftains. Other negotiated exchanges might arise along the so-called Silk Road, or the network of trade routes connecting east and southern Eurasia to the Black and Mediterranean seas as well as to the northern forest region. Trade in luxury and prestige goods had moved from east to west (intersecting with north–south routes along the way), through various intermediaries, for millennia. At the height of the Tang and Turk empires, central Asian commerce was dominated by Sogdians, an Iranian-speaking people of the Ferghana valley (western Turkistan). Sogdian merchants established trading communities throughout the region and into northern China; they also supplied officials for nomadic state builders. Traders brought their religions with their goods along these same routes, usually from west to east. Nomads figured either as mercenaries hired to protect merchant caravans or as patrons of merchants during eras when they exerted political influence through states or powerful confederations such as the Xiongnu at the turn of the first millennium, the Turk empires of the sixth century to the eighth century, the Qara Khitai of the twelfth century, and the Mongols.

Scholars continue to study and debate the exact mechanism and impact of nomadic participation in transcontinental Eurasian trade. This participation has given rise to interpretations of nomadic state formation as a solution to the economic deficiencies of pastoral nomadism, and to stereotypes of the nomad as greedy and luxury-loving, a formula particularly popular among Chinese statesmen, whose vast continental frontier assured them much experience negotiating with their northern and western neighbors. The latter charge, if true, should reassure us that nomads were like everyone else; the former requires more careful scrutiny.

Tribes and States

Nomads did not need states, it is often asserted. So why did they arise? The formation of nomadic states or confederations rested on profound changes in the structure of pastoral society. Eurasian pastoral nomads typically organized themselves into families, who shared a tent; camping groups of several families and their dependents, not always related, who shared a campfire; and patrilineal clans, whose members claimed descent from a common male ancestor. Given the circumstances of life, in which adult sons and their wives usually left the parental tent and struck out on their own with a portion of the herd, commoners did not often sustain highly structured clans or cohesive kinship units. Rather, they came together with other nomads to cooperate in pursuing common aims: defense of herds, organization of migration routes, marriage exchange, and raiding other people. We may call such groupings *tribes*. Leaders of ambition recruited members who shared their vision and granted them a kind of fictive kinship in an evolving tribe. As Rudi Lindner succinctly defines it, "the medieval Eurasian nomadic tribe was a political organism open to all who were willing to subordinate themselves to its chief and who shared interests with its tribesmen." Tribes brought together people who might belong to different ethnic and linguistic as well as kin groups; even non-nomads found their way into nomadic tribes, often but not always as captives.

Tribal formation projected nomad power outward against foes; thus, some kind of external pressure or threat (such as animal theft or attacks by other nomads) usually initiated the organization of tribes. A successful tribal leader became skilled in mediating between threatening external forces and his tribal followers, who constituted the military power that backed his mediations. When and how such tribes joined together to form supratribal federations, or nomadic states, generally involves a complex of factors, both internal and external.

Nomadic states emerged many times over the course of the last two millennia, each state sharing certain characteristics but distinct from the preceding one. Historians for long did not observe significant differences among them, with the exception of the Mongols, and have tended to view them as either "outside of history" or triggered by developments in neighboring sedentary societies. Seeking to reintegrate the history of nomadic states into world history and provide a more satisfying interpretation of their development, Nicola Di Cosmo offers a useful periodization of nomadic state formation with an analysis of its causal factors. Most crucially, he posits that inner Asian states formed in response to a crisis signaled by the disintegration of normal social relationships and tribal ties, often but not always related to nomads' persistent economic vulnerability and the chronic instability in their lives.

Rising tensions between dominant and subordinate groups, a traditional leader's loss of legitimacy, social breakdown, and detribalization encouraged increased social mobility and the emergence of rival armies headed by militarily ambitious chieftains, who recruited tightly organized personal bodyguards around them. The more young men left their herding families to join these armed units, the greater the need and hence pressure to obtain external resources to sustain them. Military competition narrowed the field of rivals down to the most ambitious, able, and charismatic men.

Investiture of a new supratribal khan, to use the ancient Turkic title for an inner Asian ruler, invoked venerable notions of heavenly favor and brought a new state into being, one which drew upon and refined historical precedents to justify itself and reorganize its basic institutions. Thus, nomadic state builders consciously, if not always explicitly, built on the experience of their predecessors, preserved in cultural memories (e.g., oral traditions and engraved monuments of past rulers), while adapting those precedents to the needs and knowledge of their own time. To assure the loyalties of his evolving centralized military apparatus, a khan had to secure the means of rewarding its members. Di Cosmo perceives that "the political centers of steppe empires were enormously expensive. The first 'cry' of a newly born inner Asian state was one of great, insatiable hunger." This hunger propelled nomadic armies outward in search of booty beyond the productive capacity of the pastoral economy. It was in the hunt for revenues that nomadic states differentiated themselves over time and evolved in both their internal organization and relationship with sedentary civilization.

In Di Cosmo's periodization, the earliest nomadic states relevant to our discussion, the Xiongnu and their immediate successors (early third century BCE to sixth century CE), relied mainly on tribute exacted from China through treaty. Subsequent nomadic empires of the sixth to tenth centuries—the Turk, Tibetan, Uighur, and Khazar—expanded their repertoire of revenue enhancement strategies to include partnerships with merchants engaged in transcontinental trade; they also tried to establish control over the trading routes between China and western Eurasia (the Silk Road). Following them, the nomadic or quasinomadic states of the Khitan Liao (predecessors of the Mongols), Tangut Xia (successors of the Tibetans), Jurchen Jin (predecessors of the later Manchus and successors of the Khitan Liao), and the early Mongols under Chinggis Khan and his first two successors conquered bits of China and added indirect taxation of farmers to tribute collection and trade. (Tribute, it should be noted, was collected from nomads as well as non-nomads.) They accomplished this by adapting earlier techniques and innovating dual structures of government to serve the different populations, agricultural and pastoral or nomadic (such dual systems appeared in west Asia as well as east Asia).

Personnel serving in these structures often had previous experience in conquest situations or were former nomads themselves, such as the Uighurs, and therefore were familiar with the traditions of both steppe and sown. In addition to deputizing merchants as tax collectors or tax farmers and administrators, inner Asian state builders might leave local rulers in place under an agent of the central regime. Double-staffing of offices was another feature of inner Asian governance in this stage.

When Khubilai Khan (r. 1260–1294) redirected the center of Mongol operations from Mongolia to north China, he inaugurated a fourth revenue-generating strategy and phase in the development of Eurasian nomadic states: direct taxation of and rule over sedentary subjects. The Mongol turning point, for Di Cosmo's time line, is not Chinggis Khan's coronation in 1206, but Khubilai's accession to the grand khan's throne in 1260. The new orientation involved heavy use of outside experts along with local officials (double-staffing) and tended to engender ethnic rivalry and jurisdictional confusion. Khubilai's Yuan Empire was not terribly adept at ruling Chinese farmers, and its residual nomadic loyalties introduced a chronic instability into Yuan politics that irreparably undermined Mongol government in the 1350s. The later Manchus, who ruled eastern Eurasia as the Qing dynasty (1644–1912), and the Ottomans, who ruled large parts of western Eurasia over roughly the same span of time, were far more effective at the direct taxation strategy. Both were deeply indebted to Mongol governing techniques.

Scholars have often remarked that the rise of the Manchu and Ottoman states, along with the Russian Romanovs, marked the closing off of central Asia; Eurasia's transcontinental trade routes entered a long decline, yielding to new maritime empires from the sixteenth century onward. The decline of overland trade relative to the explosion of maritime activity did not spell an end to the Eurasian trade. For the peoples of central Asia and their neighbors on all sides, overland trade has continued to shape economic and cultural exchange in significant ways up to the present.

Looking at Eurasian nomadic empires from the perspective of evolving strategies of revenue enhancement to resolve societal crises suggests ways in which the history of pastoral nomads is not so alien to that of sedentary civilizations. It also offers avenues of exploring the internal dynamics of nomadic states and societies for their own historical patterns of development, which cannot be ignored or divorced from any understanding of their alleged impact on sedentary societies.

Our next task is to set the geographical and historical stage on which these dramas unfolded in Eurasia.

Eurasia: Inner Eurasia, Central Asia, Inner Asia

The term *Eurasia* broadly refers to the landmass connecting Beijing and Budapest, and more specifically to the sparsely inhabited plains, mountains, deserts, and steppes stretching from Hungary to northern China (see Maps 2.1, 6.1, 7.1 and 8.1). Within that huge continental expanse, scholars speak of various overlapping subregions: inner Eurasia (the most inclusive), central Asia (the interior), and inner Asia (the regions bordering China).

Inner Eurasia contains central and inner Asia in the broadest senses. It is best pictured as a series of horizontal layers or zones, stretching from west to east. The northern most layer of permafrost (tundra) and forest (taiga, from Turkic "rocky mountain"), mostly in Siberia, does not directly concern us, although it was home to some key members of the Mongolian federation. A broad uninterrupted grass belt of steppe lands that stretch from the plains of Hungary to northeast China (Manchuria) lies south of the tundra. The Tibetan and Iranian plateaux and the Middle Eastern deserts stand at its southern edges. The word *steppe* (Russian *step'*, lowland) denotes this dry grassy plain, intermittently wooded; by extension *steppe* denotes Eurasian nomadic civilization, in contrast to the sown or sedentary world. In literature, the contrast is at times pejorative, at other times romantic or nostalgic. From the ancient Greeks on, sedentary writers typically imagined central Asia (inner Eurasia) as endless empty space periodically spewing forth hordes of savage warriors to torment the farmers of China, India, Persia, or eastern Europe. Within this zone there are few natural barriers to movement, and thus people, goods, and ideas passed relatively unhindered across vast distances. Nomadic pastoral cultures arose and spread through this wide prairie belt from the second millennium BCE on.

Central Asia: Eurasia's Heartland

Since the late twentieth century and the end of the cold war, central Asia is often understood more narrowly as the former Soviet republics of the Tajiks, Turkmens, Uzbeks, Kirghiz, and Kazakhs, along with the Chinese Xinjiang Uighur Autonomous Region, that is, what used to be called western and eastern Turkistan. The area encompasses two ecological zones: steppe and desert, with gradations of each and lots of mountains along the southern perimeter. Central Asia forms an enclosed, arid region with no outlet to the world's oceans. All of its rivers flow into the interior and drain into deserts or lakes. Temperatures fluctuate dramatically and strong winds whip up without warning. Historical geographers have sometimes identified the fluctuating water or temperature levels as determining the rise and fall of civilization in the region. Indeed, such theories have attempted to explain the fortunes of Chinggis Khan, though they have not gained many adherents.

Some definitions of central Asia exclude Kazakhstan, which lies squarely in the steppe belt, and describe the region as mostly desert–oases habitat, highlighting the significant differences between steppe and desert. Desert habitat favored a civilization based on irrigated agriculture and trade or the Turk–Tadjik symbiosis of Mahmud Kashgari, which was characteristic of central and southwest Asia and the Middle East. Steppe habitat fostered a civilization based on pastoral nomadism in which humans depended largely on herding and hunting (with limited farming), and traded or raided for other essential goods. Nomads' livelihood, as we have seen, involved seasonal migration to summer and winter pastures, and required mobility, adaptability, and a particular style of leadership.

Inner Asia: The East Asian Perimeter of Eurasia

In most categorizing schemes, Mongolia falls outside central Asia and into the inner Asian zone around China that includes Tibet, Manchuria, and eastern Turkistan (Chinese Xinjiang), the latter now part of the People's Republic of China. Mongolia's grasslands lie in the often well-watered valleys of its forested mountains; its rivers flow north into Siberia and south into China. Rocky semidesert, or Gobi, covers much of southern Mongolia. Mongolia's history, however, gives it an equally strong westward orientation: the Mongolian steppes gave birth to the great medieval nomadic empires including the old Turk confederation of the sixth and seventh centuries, whose collapse sent its members outward to Eurasia's western perimeter. When the Mongols ruled over China, they reigned as grand khans of a Eurasian empire, not merely as

Chinese emperors. When Mongolia became the world's second communist nation in 1921, it participated in the cultural and economic world of Europe's eastern bloc countries. Culturally and politically, today's Mongols seek membership in a broader Eurasian community beyond the economic shadow of giant China.

At the eastern end of central Asia, along the inner Asian frontiers of China, the nomadic–sedentary relationship displayed the full spectrum from accommodation to hostility, although Chinese writers, especially Confucian scholar-officials, emphasized the hostility and nomads' dependence on handouts. The Great Wall of China, as we have it today, was built in the sixteenth century and extensively repaired in the late twentieth century. A powerful and complex symbol, before the thirteenth century it was less a product of nomadic–sedentary hostility than it was of a state-building process that defined the winners in intramural struggles for power on the north China plain. Over the centuries, inner Asians regularly participated in those struggles for power and about half the time won them. Textbooks are beginning to acknowledge that the historical development of China is not simply a tale of indigenous Han peoples defending their lands against rapacious nomads, but rather the gradual symbiosis of inner Asian specialists in warfare and trade with east Asian specialists in literate bureaucracy and taxation, as John King Fairbank argues in his last work, *China, A New History*.

It is the Turks who linked eastern and western Eurasia in the twelfth century. Arising in Mongolia, at one end of Eurasia, migrating through central Asia and centuries later settling in what became Turkey at the other end, now half European half Eurasian, the Turks paved the way for the Mongols.

The Turkic Migrations and the Southern Russian Steppes

Turks played a leading role in the Mongol Empire; they were culturally and linguistically close to the Mongols and numbered among the members of Chinggis Khan's federation. Their ancestors provided models of nomadic tribal confederation and empire. A general overview of the situation of the Turks will give the reader a deeper understanding of the world in which Chinggis Khan lived and the impact of his life.

The adjective *Turkic* used here refers to a shared linguistic and cultural heritage; *Turkish* denotes the attributes and inhabitants of the modern country of Turkey, a product of the Ottoman Empire, and thus does not feature much in this narrative. The Turkic languages belong to the Altaic language family, whose members include Manchu (Jurchen) and Mongolic. The word *Turkic* covers a great many peoples and groups over time, but their shared linguistic ties, origins, and experiences give them a distinct historical and cultural identity, certainly with respect to the non-Turkic peoples with whom they came into contact.

With the collapse of the first great medieval Turk Empire in the seventh century, northern India, Persia, and western Eurasia received successive waves of

Turkic-speaking immigrants eddying out from the steppes of northern Asia. These nomads often supplanted or absorbed older groups as they moved west and south, peopling the backyards of the urban civilizations ringing the Old World. The long history of Turkic migrations, sketched largely in negative stereotypes by hostile settled folks, is a history of ethnogenesis and state formation. It is also a history of the gradual linguistic Turkicization of Eurasia, such that today if you travel overland from Hungary to China, in your daily interactions with local people you would find it very useful to know one of the major Turkic languages, Uzbek, for example.

The cleverest among the migrants found jobs for their followers as hired mercenaries, tax collectors, and bodyguards for insecure princes or sultans; sometimes they took over the throne. The less successful fell back on raiding nearby towns. Turkic peoples became a principal target of slave raiders, who delivered their human booty to the flourishing slave markets of western Eurasia. Many Turks entered the armies of regional Islamic rulers as "military slaves" and enjoyed a relatively high status. Some "slaves" went on to found their own dynasties, notably the Mamluks in Egypt.

Their dynasties seldom lasted long, given the traditional love of horse-riding pastoralists for autonomy and mobility. Whereas the absence of strong centralized authority among Turkic groups made them difficult neighbors at times, pressures from other nomadic groups made them unpredictable military allies, as the Russian princes came to understand. Still, nomads formed marital and trading alliances with their host societies and integrated with the local inhabitants. Such interactions occurred regularly in the southern Russian steppes, before and throughout the Mongol era, hence the expression, "scratch a Russian, find a Tartar."

As the Turks converted to Islam through contact with towns, merchants, and Sufi missionaries along the central Asian trade routes, they began to form more complex, hybrid polities around urban centers. Nomads slowly turned into merchants. Islam spread not by the sword but by the strong attraction of its rich and vibrant civilization to the peoples on its margins. Islam indeed eased the process of Turkicization in central Asia by blurring ethnic lines. Islamicized Turkic state builders had to fend off raids by newer non-Islamic Turkic immigrant groups, as they in turn encroached on older Arab Muslim states.

The Seljuks, whose invasions into Anatolia sparked the First Crusade, exemplified this pattern. The Seljuk state was a Turkic tribal union with a weakly centralized authority divided among various princes and their Iranian bureaucratic advisors. Collectively but rarely in concert, they extended this authority west and southwest at the expense of other Muslim Arab states (Egypt and Syria) as well as the Byzantine Empire in the eleventh and twelfth centuries. One result was the gradual Turkicization and Islamicization of Anatolia. On the eve of the Mongol invasions, it is estimated that up to a million Turkic folk had settled in the towns and countryside across Anatolia. The outpost of Seljukid rule here, the Sultanate of Rum (ostensible target of the First Crusade), reached its peak right before the last Mongol invasions of Europe.

The domain of the Kievan princes of Rus', rulers of the eastern Slavs, lay north of the Black Sea or Pontic steppes, which had been occupied since at least the eighth century by diverse nomadic federations. Struggle with nomads forms a recurring motif in Kievan historiography and Orthodox Church writings. Long and intimate contact resulted in a certain degree of steppe influence on Kievan politics and culture. By the mid-eleventh century, a powerful new influx of nomads, the Qipchaqs (called Polovsty in Russian sources and Cumans in Latin ones), set up a confederation in the Pontic steppes that lasted until the Mongol absorption of this region over a hundred years later. The multiethnic, multilingual Qipchaq federation absorbed many people flung westward by the collapse in the 1120s of the great Khitan Empire north of China. It featured no central authority and its nobles, like their predecessors, became drawn into Kievan society and princely infighting through marriage and other alliances. References in Rus' chronicles to Polovtsian raids often really mask eruptions of civil war among the Kievan princes, and both sides raided each other for various sorts of booty.

After Kiev's conversion to Orthodox Christianity in the tenth century, its relations with the nomads took on a militantly Russophilic tone in Church writings. When the dreaded Mongol–Tatars showed up in the 1220s, Kievan churchmen went on writing about the nomads in the same way, only more so, in effect concealing the important political role that the Mongols came to play in relations among the Kievan princes. Charles Halperin has termed this the *ideology of silence*, a denial of the fact of conquest. However one chooses to analyze it, however different their relationship with these new nomads in fact turned out to be, it did not alter a basic and difficult fact for the Russians: neither of Europe nor of the steppe, they absorbed from both and yet remained apart. They even remained apart from the Mongol Empire, an insignificant source of sustained booty extracted via taxation by the Mongol princes who ruled the Golden Horde in the steppes north of the Black and Caspian seas.

Other Turkic peoples gave rise to two empires that, in the year 1200, set the stage for Chinggis Khan's enterprise and marked the unstable frontier between a Turko-Iranian Dar al-Islam (Islamic world) and a non-Islamic Turko-Chinese world: Khwarazm, at the southwest corner of the steppe belt, and the Qara Khitai, a mixed nomadic–sedentary empire spanning most of central Asia up to present-day Xinjiang, in western China. The Mongols collapsed this seeming religious frontier into their "world empire."

Turks Between Central and East Asia: Khwarazm and Qara Khitai

Khwarazm names an ancient Iranian trade emporium centered in the fertile lowland region of the river Amu Darya, where it flows into the Aral Sea along the sea's southern shore. (In Greek sources, the Amu Darya is called the *Oxus*, and the region between this river and the Syr Darya, or Jaxartes River, which empties into the Aral on its northeast shore, is called *Transoxania*, "across the Oxus.") From this emporium the products of the northern forests (furs and timber) flowed to the Islamic world and entered the stream of trade along the transcontinental networks comprising the Silk Route. An outpost of Persian civilization along the steppe frontier, Khwarazm fell under Seljuk sway in the eleventh century. In the twelfth century, the Turkic shahs of Khwarazm ostensibly served as provincial governors for the Seljuks. Their power and hold on the region increased after the last great Seljuk sultan lost a key battle in 1141 with the founder of the expanding Qara Khitai Empire, Yelu Dashi.

Yelu Dashi's momentous defeat of the Seljuk sultan Sanjar in 1141 echoed in the courts of Europe as a Nestorian (eastern Christian) crusade against the infidel, spawning rumors of a Christian king in Asia by the name of Prester John. (Yelu Dashi, we might note, was Buddhist, not Christian.) In 1200 an ambitious and imperious new shah came to the Khwarazmian throne. 'Ala al-Din Muhammad II proceeded to enlarge his domain, conquering much of present-day central and eastern Iran and Afghanistan. He also wrested Transoxania (locally called Mawarannahr, the land between the rivers Amu Darya and Syr Darya) from the Qara Khitai in 1210 and moved his capital to its most famous city, Samarqand. Muhammad had grand designs but he proved unprepared for the challenge awaiting him farther east.

Although fewer sources remain to tell their story, the people who established the Qara Khitai Empire exerted a profound influence over twelfth-century Asia. They prolonged by almost a hundred years the imperial history of the Khitan clan, which founded an empire in northeastern Asia in the early tenth century. Those Khitans, a Mongolic-speaking nomadic people, incorporated a significant population inhabiting the northern fringe of China, and then evolved a distinctive dual form of government to administer their nomadic and settled subjects, in which Chinese managed the sedentary population, and Khitans or other nomads governed the nomadic elements. They took the Chinese dynastic name of Liao (907–1125), from the Chinese name of the river (Shira Muren) where their origins lay in southwestern Manchuria. In documents written in their own script, however, they called their state the Qara Khitai, or "Black" Khitai, the adjective *black* thought to be equivalent to *great*.

In the early eleventh century, the Liao Khitans had negotiated a military and diplomatic accommodation with the Chinese Song dynasty; by treaty Song China supplied the Khitans with annual payments of silk and silver in exchange for peace. This Chinese capital greased the wheels of Khitan commerce with the central Asian peoples to their west and southwest, and gave the world several names for China: Cathay (from *Khitai*), Marco Polo's name for China; and *Khitai* (from the Turkic variant of Khitan), the Russian name for China. For the Turkic world of inner Eurasia, the Khitans were China.

In the 1120s the Liao collapsed, overthrown by one of its subject peoples. Remnants of its court fled north into Mongolia and then west into central Asia under a royal scion, the same Yelu Dashi, who established the western Liao or Qara Khitai state, as it is usually called, and gradually conquered significant Muslim territories up to the Aral Sea. Yelu Dashi was an extraordinary figure who rose to an extraordinary challenge. Raised and educated in both the Chinese and Khitan traditions, as befitted a Liao aristocrat, he proved himself a warrior par excellence and a brilliant political strategist. His skills, if not his background, foreshadowed those of his Mongol successors; he operated deftly in many cultural and ecological environments and commanded the loyalties of diverse tribal groups, exemplifying the adaptability and initiative that steppe traditions bred in their leaders. The new state continued many of the dual practices pioneered by the Khitans in governing their former multiethnic empire, and most of the ruling class remained Buddhist.

Michal Biran calls the Liao and Qara Khitai aristocrats Sino-Khitans (i.e., Chinese-Khitans) to acknowledge their complex cultural identity. In the eyes of Muslim authors, the Khitans appeared as a fusion of Turk and Chinese identities. The Qara Khitai rulers played the Chinese card to capitalize on the awe and mystery in which their new Muslim subjects and neighbors beheld China. Some Muslim writers call them Turks or "infidel Turks" or "Khitan Turks." A fifteenth-century Muslim source even refers to them as *Tatars*, all of these instances indicating tendencies to conflate the Qara Khitans with some of their subject peoples or with the Mongols who followed them.

Liao's former upstart vassals, the Jurchens, went on to set up their own dynasty, the Jin or "Golden" (Altan, in Turko-Mongolian) state, which dominated northern Asia until it fell to Chinggis Khan's generals in 1234. The Jurchens spoke an early form of Manchu and were a forest people rather than a steppe people. They are considered the ancestors of the tribal federation which conquered all of China in the mid-seventeenth century under the self-invented name of Manchu. The Jurchens expanded southward to take over all of north China from the Song dynasty in 1127, pushing the Chinese south to reestablish their capital at Hangzhou, a Yangzi delta city.

The Khitans were a Mongolic-speaking people and may be considered the immediate ancestors of the Mongols. But although sharing a linguistic and nomadic heritage with the Mongols, the Khitans differed from them in one crucial respect, which recalls the question of the difference between steppe and desert habits in central Asia and its significance for our story. The Turks we have been talking about, and the Khitans, had a history of gradual adaptation to desert and settled habitats in central, northeast, and southwest Asia. They had learned how to value and employ the resources of other habitats, notably their commercial potential. Most Turks still looked down on farmers, but had come to understand that farmers were the basis of steady incomes for rulers and merchants. Also, rulers could delegate the task of dealing with farmers and extracting their taxable surpluses to the class of literate bureaucrats always eager to advise the throne (especially in China and Persia). This seeming piece of common sense had involved a fundamental shift in consciousness and social behavior. Not all Turks in any given group made the shift at the same time: the first to do so were those with political ambitions, but it was useful, after all, to keep loyal bands of warriors to guard or expand the booty base. By 1220, this process had been at work among the Turks and Khitans for hundreds of years. For the Mongols, it took place in a few decades, even within one lifetime, for the more astute chieftains. The time crunch may explain the destructive aspect of the Mongols' early invasions and occupation policies. But the Mongols were very fast learners.

One last characteristic of the Eurasian stage merits comment. From the earlier discussion it should be abundantly clear that cultural identity on the steppe was fluid but not formless. Mobility and adaptability, necessary for survival, made nomads flexible and pragmatic. Livelihood and experience and loyalty to chiefs defined one's identity and culture more than bloodline, native tongue, or even religion. Islamicized nomads continued to venerate their Heaven (Tengri) and consult shamans. A bounded piece of territory carried no particular import, although people, animals, mountains, water, and pasture did. As pastoral groups moved through space, they adapted to new social and linguistic environments, absorbed new members, picked up new skills, learned new songs, passed on old stories with new names. What it meant to be Mongol, for example, proves very difficult to pin down in the terms familiar to us from our own census categories or the late twentieth-century understandings of culture and ethnicity. For Mongols, if not for their Chinese or Persian subjects, identity of significance was ecological and political, defined more in terms of relationship to one's environment and to the khan than to one's father's birthplace.

What it meant to be born in twelfth-century Mongolia, destined to become Chinggis Khan, is the subject of Chapter 2.

CHAPTER

2

Origins of Chinggis Khan: Mongolia in the Twelfth Century

At the beginning there was a blue-grey wolf, born with his destiny ordained by Heaven Above.

—THE SECRET HISTORY OF THE MONGOLS

The remote deserts, steppes, and forested mountains north of China and south of Lake Baikal were home to a scattered population of pastoral nomads who made a living mainly by herding the "five snouts," hunting, and raiding one another. They migrated along fairly stable seasonal routes to well-watered and wind-sheltered pastures. Sheep, goats, and cattle provided their main source of food and clothing in the form of dairy products, skins, and fur; horses and camels served as an essential means of transport. Of these animals, sheep offered the most in sustaining life, but horses held the highest symbolic value and their ownership distinguished nomads of means and ambition from mere survivors.

Archaeology and history show that in favorable pockets of watered land, some pastoralists also grew cereal crops, but in the main the nomads of the Mongolian plateau had to trade with other folk for grain, tea, cotton or silk textiles, and metal implements. Nomads dwelling near the major Eurasian trade routes linking north China and central Asia with entrepots farther west engaged more extensively in trade than their northern neighbors. Such activities yielded valuable contacts with the wider world that furnished information as well as material goods, all of which fostered a higher degree of social stratification and thus political development among those nomads. People who controlled the trade tended to have more social and political power. In the twelfth century, the Mongols did not yet figure among those people.

Early Accounts

In a mythical account preserved in the thirteenth-century *Secret History of the Mongols*, the Mongols' ancestral genealogy begins with the union of a blue-gray wolf and fallow doe. Striking similarities with the ancient Turk-origin legends prompt Igor de Rachewiltz to reason that the imperial Mongols borrowed the Turk tale, which would have circulated widely on the steppe, and recast their own origins in the apt royal garb of those glorious conquerors of bygone years. Among the offspring of the Mongols' totemic progenitors figures a man whose wife, Alan Gho'a, becomes a matrilineal link in the chain of descent, bearing three sons after her husband's death. The founders of branches of the Mongols' chief Borjigin lineage descend from these miraculous children. Alan Gho'a's domestic tribulations echo and anticipate the important role played by the mother and the wife of Chinggis Khan in the *Secret History*, and the prominent position of women in the Mongolian Empire. In the mytho-history of the Mongols, these three women champion family values, the unity and cooperation of brothers against a hostile world being chief among them. What we know of the real story tells us that brothers typically fought or plotted against one another.

Early Chinese versions of the name *Mongol* first show up in Tang dynasty (618–907 CE) sources to denote one member of a larger confederation. The Mongols we are concerned about are also sometimes classified in Chinese sources as "Black" or "Raw Tatars," in contrast to the more civilized (or "cooked") "White Tatars" to their south. From Chinese sources we learn that in the tenth century, the early Mongols had migrated west and south from the Amur River area (northern Manchuria) to settle between the Onon and Kerulen rivers in northeastern Mongolia. This move from a mostly forested habitat to a mixed area of forest and steppe led the Mongols to take up herding, especially of camels and sheep, and become pastoralists, although hunting supplemented and sometimes replaced reliance on domesticated flocks.

Emergence into History

The Mongols might have migrated out of Manchuria (see Map 2.1) in response to the rise of the mighty Liao Empire in the tenth century, forged by the Khitans, another northeastern Mongolic-speaking people whose ethnonym for centuries ever after meant "China" (Khitai–Cathay) to the farther West. Liao supremacy in northern Asia profoundly reshaped relationships among the steppe peoples who became their subjects. In the late eleventh century the name *Mongol* appears in reference to a remote tribe that paid tribute to the Khitans. By the early twelfth century, when the Liao Empire collapsed, Chinese records tended to lump together leading Mongol clans with their older and more powerful enemies, the Tatars, to the southeast, while other clans who later became "Mongols" appear as separate groups. Thus there is no fixed referent for the name Mongol and even the people most closely associated with that name did not always use it to refer to themselves.

When the Jurchens of Manchuria overthrew their Liao masters and replaced the Khitans as overlords of the northern steppe (and all of north China) in the 1120s, the Tatars and other smaller tribes entered into service as frontier wardens for the new Jurchen Jin (Gold) dynasty (1115–1234), helping them to keep the northern tribes "pacified." For the Tatars, this relationship yielded wealth, through gifts and trade, and prestige vis-à-vis other nomads. Tatar wealth also derived from the proximity of their migration routes to silver mines.

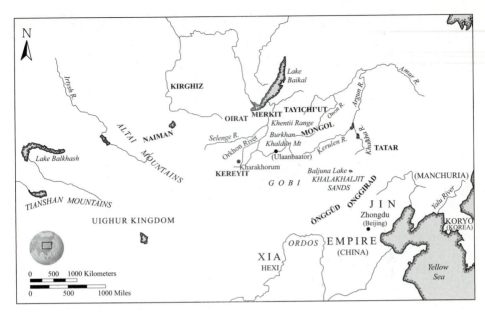

Map 2.1 Mongolia and North Asia in the twelfth Century

These developments stimulated the aspirations of the Mongols, farther north, to advance their position in the frontier pecking order, and they sought to organize and compete with the Tatars in order to negotiate a better deal with the Jurchens. In the early years of Jin rule, Mongol-led groups attacked Jurchen fortifications with some success, gaining the attention of the Jin emperor. Khabul Khan emerged in Mongol oral tradition as the earliest chieftain over all the Mongols, and so found himself a guest at the Jin emperor's coronation in 1125. His lack of courtly graces (according to the Chinese version of the story, he tugged the emperor's beard) appalled the courtiers, though not the monarch, himself a seasoned warrior. The former had him chased home; Khabul Khan eluded his pursuers but Mongol cavalry began attacking Jin armies and forts, inflicting serious damage in the 1140s. The two sides came to terms in 1147, by which Jin supplied the Mongols with quantities of cattle, sheep, foodstuffs, and silk, and awarded a fancy title to their leader.

The Jurchens, naturally, found this arrangement humiliating and turned to fomenting antagonism between Mongols and Tatars as a way to punish the upstart northern tribesmen. Khabul Khan was succeeded by a cousin, Ambaghai, whom the Tatars betrayed to Jurchen agents during a marriage negotiation. Before his delivery to the Jurchen, who had Ambaghai nailed to a wooden donkey, the prisoner secreted a message back home, exhorting his followers to seek vengeance for his death. Khabul's son Khutula inherited the khan-ship and the command, and though he led many lucrative raids against the Jin, he fared poorly in the struggle with the Tatars.

Thus efforts to unify the tribes collapsed in the early 1160s, following a Tatar victory that left Khutula slain. While Temüjin (the future Chinggis Khan) was growing up in the later decades of the twelfth century, the Mongols were obliged to pay tribute to the Jurchens even as Tatar–Jurchen raids supplied Mongol slaves to Jin markets. In this fashion Jin tried to weaken the tribes, sowing the seeds of enmity between Tatars and Mongols in the fertile ground that framed the early years of Temüjin's life. Undoubtedly the rivalry and enmity between Tatars and Mongols fed the crisis that, in Di Cosmo's model of inner Asian state formation, lay at the heart of Chinggis Khan's rise to power.

Neighbors and Rivals

Somewhat west of Tatar–Mongol territory, the Kereyits, traditional rivals to the Tatars, played out their own dramas in the heartland of the old Turkic empires, the Orkhon River in central Mongolia. Kereyit khans held court there in splendid golden tents and commanded large armies. The most politically centralized of all the tribes on the plateau, they had, moreover, converted to Nestorian Christianity a century earlier, as a result of close ties with the urbane Uighur Turk trading communities in eastern central Asia. Kereyit sophistication stemmed from commercial and diplomatic relationships cultivated with merchants and ruling houses in central Asia and north China, in particular the Qara Khitai and Tangut Xia, respectively. In the mid-twelfth century a Kereyit khan had once sought assistance from the Naimans in western Mongolia, the third and probably most powerful tribal confederation on the plateau at that time, normally not friends of the Kereyits. Because a principal way to bolster support was through marital exchange, the father of the Kereyit protagonist of this tale, Toghril or Ong-khan, had a Naiman wife whose two sons vied with Ong-khan and his brothers for succession to the Kereyit throne. Toghril's relations with the Naimans were understandably hostile. The resulting instability played an important part in the rise of Temüjin.

For their part, royal power in the Naiman realm, divided physically by the Altai Mountains, often broke apart between brothers sharing the throne and had passed its peak by the close of the twelfth century. Unlike the Kereyits, Tatars, and Mongols, the Naimans were Turkic-speaking and had developed literacy and record-keeping. Like the Kereyits, some of their elite had adopted Nestorian Christianity. The Naimans considered themselves vastly superior to the comparatively backward Mongols, as well as to everyone else.

The fourth player among the tribal groups on the plateau were the Merkits of northern Mongolia's forested fringe, along the lower reaches of the Selenge River before it flows into Lake Baikal. The Merkits practiced some agriculture along with herding, had no organized leadership or khan, and bitterly resisted the Mongol unification under Chinggis Khan. The threads of feuding and revenge between Mongols and Merkits, and between Mongols and Tatars, lend bold colors to the fabric of this story. We pick up that thread later with the history of Yisügei, father of Chinggis Khan.

Social Crisis on the Mongolian Plateau

Following the collapse of early Mongol efforts to unite under a strong khan, constant raids, plundering, and general chaos in the post-1160 era led to the impoverishment or enslavement of many Mongols and a disintegration of the clan-based social order. Customarily, tribes and their constituent lineages were fluid entities, created more by alliance than by biological reproduction, and held together by common purpose and rituals of fictive kinship. The Mongols, like most of their neighbors, distinguished among nobles, commoners, and dependents. Nobles included the founders of clan lineages and any descendants advancing claims to leadership; commoners tended to be their junior relatives. Dependents counted people captured in raids or battles with other nomads or settled peoples (whole lineages could be thus enslaved), who had to work for their new masters but were often treated as family members. Mongols married exogamously, outside their patrilines, often establishing a marriage exchange with another patrilineage. In ca. 1140, the Mongol chiefly clan, the Borjigin, began taking wives from another prominent clan in eastern Mongolia, the Onggirat, thus acquiring allies against the Tatars. Eventually the Mongols absorbed this people into their tribal alliance as the in-law clan of the royal Chinggisids. Both the mother and the wife of Chinggis Khan came from Onggirat sublineages, although many Onggirats resisted the Borjigin drive for leadership over the Mongol clans until 1203.

In the late twelfth century, the population of the territory of present-day Mongolia was quite sparse, probably numbering no more than seven hundred thousand. The key to power and wealth, therefore, lay not in control over land, but over people. Disorder and warfare in twelfth-century Mongolia inspired a lot of young men to leave their lineages and form new alliances, in search of a strong leader. Youths attracted to a likely candidate became *nököd*, or companions, voluntary followers forming a would-be chieftain's retinue of advisers, errand-runners, loyal warriors, and an essential part of his household. Nököd might be nobles or slaves; they were never related to their masters. In return they expected an equal share of any benefits accruing to the alliance, principally in the form of war booty. This social element became the basis of Chinggis Khan's rise to power and helps us appreciate the fruitless albeit eloquent appeals to family unity in the *Secret History*.

Many sources remember the debased living conditions of the Mongols at that time. In the vivid words of thirteenth-century Persian chronicler Juvaini,

> Each tribe or two tribes lived separately; they were not united with one another, and there was constant fighting and hostility between them. Some of them regarded robbery and violence, immorality and debauchery as deeds of manliness and excellence. The Khan of Khitai [Jin ruler] used to demand and seize goods from them. Their clothing was of the skins of dogs and mice, and their food was the flesh of those animals and other dead things; their wine was mares' milk and their dessert the fruit of a tree shaped like the pine . . . besides which no other fruit-bearing tree will grow in that region. . . . The sign of a great emir amongst them was that his stirrups were of iron; from which one can form a picture of their other luxuries. And they continued in this indigence, privation and misfortune until the banner of Chingiz-Khan's fortune was raised. . . .

Juvaini may not have realized that the Khitans and Jurchens embargoed the export of iron to the steppe, for obvious security reasons. Under such scarcity, iron stirrups would become a luxury available only to those with clout.

In the *Secret History*, an intimate family friend chastised the elder sons of Chinggis as they quarreled over the paternity of one of them: "Before you were born, the starry sky was turning upon itself, the many people were in turmoil: they did not enter beds to rest, but fought against each other. . . . At such time your mother was abducted. It was not her wish: It happened at a time when men met, weapons in hand. . . ."

Yisügei Ba'atur

Chinggis Khan's father, Yisügei the "Brave" (d. 1171?), was a grandson and nephew of the unlucky mid-twelfth century Mongol khans. He established a sublineage (the Kiyat) of the noble Borjigin clan to which he belonged, perhaps hoping himself to assume the lapsed mantle of khan-ship. This meant continuing the struggle with the Tatars, among others, who were responsible for the capture and deaths of several relatives of Yisügei. His first appearance in the *Secret History* illustrates the happenstance of everyday life in twelfth-century Mongolia. Out hunting with his falcons, he brought home not game for the stewpot but a beautiful girl-wife, captured on the fly from her husband, a noble Merkit, of the forests north of Mongol territory. Yisügei's new wife, Hö'elün, was born into an Onggirat clan and then married off to a Merkit. Her dramatic entrance into the story becomes emblematic of the unsettled conditions on the steppe, referred to vividly earlier and elsewhere to emphasize the obstacles facing the youths who grew up to bring order, peace, and glory to their people. It also gives voice to the spirited Mongol woman who became the "mother of the nation": She sends her luckless man off with her shirt as a fragrant memento and raises a loud lament while being led away by Yisügei's brothers, who tell her to shut up.

Marriage by abduction was a common practice on the steppe, given the difficulty of long-distance communications, and not solely a sign of social decay. The *Secret History* is the only source that tells the story of Hö'elün's "marriage" to Yisügei; no doubt the later Chinese and Persian court historians preferred to gloss over such crude incivility in a matter of such sociomoral weight to bureaucratic pedants raised in societies where marriages were carefully planned by one's parents. In any event, Yisügei had another wife of uncertain origin who had two sons, Begter and Belgütei, but by all accounts the role of main wife fell to Hö'elün.

Sometime after acquiring his Onggirat wife, Yisügei participated in the gathering of Mongols by the Onon River, which elected Khutula as the next khan, initiating a new cycle of warfare with the Tartars. By this time, according to Rashid al-Din, Yisügei had become a prominent chieftain among the Mongol people, though not influential enough to be picked as Khutula's successor. So he sought alliances outside his kin network and became "sworn friends" or *anda* with Toghril, the Kereyit khan. Toghril needed support in asserting his leadership against the claims of his brothers and uncles, and Yisügei helped him, probably militarily, to secure his rule. These two men's *anda*-ship became a crucial inheritance for Yisügei's son.

Figure 2.1 Khentii Landscape, land of Temujin's childhood © Ruth Dunnell/Ruth W. Dunnell.

Birth of Temüjin

It was during a battle with the Tartars that Hö'elün delivered her first child at Spleen Hill by the Onon River (see Figure 2.1). According to the *Secret History*, the boy was born clutching a blood clot the size of a knucklebone, an apt birth-mark for a child of destiny. An ancient motif in Asian folklore, possibly of Buddhist origin, the blood clot in the hand of a new-born baby announces the birth of a fierce conqueror. Knucklebones, or more likely ankle-bones of a sheep, were common toys for children, used in various games somewhat like dice or jacks up to this day, and now popular tourist souvenirs.

Yisügei named the baby after the Tatar chief he had just captured, Temüjin Öge (Ironsmith the Wise?), thereby hoping to bestow on his son the valor of his aristocratic captive. The prisoner was likely put to death after the christening, thus sealing the transfer of martial virtue from Tatar warrior to infant Mongol. As you might expect, the birth of the child who became Chinggis Khan has been embellished in every retelling, spawning cycles of legends enshrined in later liter-ary works of diverse origins.

It is impossible to say exactly when Temüjin was born; until very recently such precise dates were not meaningful to most Mongols. But after a century or more of debate, the best scholars in the field have narrowed down the possibilities to some-time between 1162 and 1167. In Mongolia his official birthdate is May 30, 1162. This account will calculate roughly on the basis of 1162 as his year of birth.

3

Education of a Hero, 1160s–1180s

We have no friend but our shadow, we have no whip but our horse's tail.

—THE SECRET HISTORY OF THE MONGOLS

The social crisis on the Mongolian plateau, as analyzed in *Secret History* and other sources inspired by it, animates the life of Temüjin. He seemed to spend much of his early life escaping from either hunger or captivity by hostile tribes. Families were unpredictable, sometimes disappearing, sources of inspiration and instability. In his travels from boyhood to adulthood, Temüjin received shelter, support, and instruction from a number of families: that of his own mother, his future wife, and various benefactors. In this story, the most reliable families become the ones you put together yourself. Temüjin could not do without his family, but ended up remaking it to suit his needs, rejecting those elements that threatened to challenge or constrain his ambitions. Survival imposed on him a sense of destiny: Find the means to transcend the circumstances of his precarious environment and bend them to his will. Survival also imposed the obligation to repay those who helped him, but that still lay in the future.

A Mongolian Childhood

When Temüjin was nine (or eight, as the Mongols, like the Chinese and other Asians, added a year to their age at the New Year), he had four full siblings: brothers Khasar (Jochi Khasar, 7), Khachi'un (5), Temüge-otchigin (3; *otchigin* referred to the youngest son, who would become "guardian or keeper of the hearth," that is, inherit his father's tents and herds and take care of his mother), and an infant sister, Temülün. The ages given in the *Secret History* seem too neat and may be symbolic; nine was an auspicious and recurring number for the Mongols and Turks (as well as for the Greeks!). The family also included stepbrothers Begter and Belgütei, the sons of Yisügei's second wife, whose ages are not given.

Temüjin and his siblings grew up along the Onon River, learning to ride, hunt birds with a bow, fish, and play games with dice made from sheep's anklebones. Temüjin played with Jamukha, an orphaned cousin of the Jadaran branch of the Borjigin lineage, who became his first blood brother or *anda*. Around 1170 or 1171, when

Temüjin was nine years old by Mongol reckoning, his father took the boy to his mother's relatives to find him a wife. Marriages were arranged early throughout Asia, the steppe being no exception. Along the way Yisügei met Dei Sechen, an Onggirat chieftain with a lively daughter, Börte, just the right age, a year or so older than Temüjin (*Börte* means "sky-blue" or "blue-gray," cf. "Celeste"). A wife's maturity was regarded as an asset to her husband. The fathers addressed each other as *khuda* (relative by marriage) in the *Secret History* and happily acknowledged that their children are ones "who have fire in their eyes, who have light in their faces," as heroes in epics and oral literature were characterized.

Rashid al-Din records a tougher marriage negotiation, with Dei Sechen's younger son obliged to put in a good word for Temüjin, whom he took to right away (and served later as a highly celebrated general). Yisügei left Temüjin at Dei Sechen's camp to work for his father-in-law, according to custom and at Dei Sechen's demand. A son-in-law's labor constituted the bride-price for nomads who had little else to give in exchange for a daughter-in-law. Yisügei had only a thin horse to leave with Temüjin, but he thus renewed an alliance with the Onggirat. Also, regardless of the "light" and "fire" in the children's countenances, in the *Secret History* Yisügei's last words to Dei Sechen—"my son is afraid of dogs. *Khuda*, don't let him be frightened by dogs!"—put a more personal seal on the arrangement. Mongol dogs were huge, ferocious beasts whose primary function was to guard the encampment and attack any unauthorized visitors. The lad's fear indicated a healthy instinct for personal survival. Someone you called *khuda*, moreover, was not simply a pesky in-law, but an important political ally. Establishing a khuda relationship could involve considerable exchange of goods and subject peoples, as occurred regularly among the Mongol conquest elite in later years.

On the way back to his own camp, Yisügei met some Tatars and shared a meal with them, as steppe hospitality commanded. By the time he reached home, he was very ill, convinced that his Tatar hosts had recognized and poisoned him. He sent an old retainer to fetch back his son, but when Temüjin arrived, Yisügei was dead. The year was probably 1171 or 1172.

In the Mongols' own telling, Temüjin's emergence as a leader following his father's demise was predicated on the extreme hardship suffered by his family. Thus, after Yisügei's death, their Tayichi'ut relatives (rivals for leadership over the Mongols) cut Hö'elün out of the ancestral ceremonies and departed for new campgrounds with Yisügei's kin and followers. Rashid al-Din depicts a less than total abandonment. The Mongol custom of levirate (practiced also by the ancient Hebrews, among other nomadic folks) would permit one of Yisügei's younger brothers, or a son by a wife other than the widow, to step in and marry his widow. So Rashid claims that Daritai-otchigin, Temüjin's uncle, and his men remained at Yisügei's camp, though it seems that Hö'elün did not remarry. Some historians have speculated that the old retainer's son, Mönglik, then probably in his twenties, became for all practical purposes Hö'elün's husband and provider. Mönglik's long association with the family and the key role played by his seven sons in Chinggis Khan's rise to power make this hypothesis attractive. The *Secret*

History, however, focuses on the isolation of the mother and her subsequent labors to keep her large family together.

This was not an easy task under the best of circumstances. Mongol histories extol Hö'elün's unstinting efforts to tame her unruly brood and rummage for food along the Onon River. The children grew up on crab apples, bird cherries, roots, wild garlic, wild onion, and lily bulbs. Nevertheless they "became handsome and good, and grew up into fine men truly valiant and bold, saying to each other, 'Let us feed our mother!' They sat on the banks of Mother Onon . . . and fished. . . ."

Brothers

If the *Secret History* dramatizes or glorifies some aspects of the future conqueror's life, it also includes episodes suppressed in other accounts as unworthy of its subject. One of these, the sibling rivalry between Temüjin and his stepbrother Begter, close in age, climaxed in an argument over a fish. One day Temüjin and Khasar ran complaining to their mother: "A shiny dace bit our hook, but it was snatched away from us by our brothers Begter and Belgütei." Hö'elün scolded the boys in words familiar to every Mongol today, "'We have no friend but our shadow, we have no whip but our horse's tail' . . . how can you be at odds with each other, like the five sons of Mother Alan of old? Stop it!"

Mother Alan of old, Alan Gho'a, had five sons, three conceived after the death of her husband by a ray of light entering the smoke hole of her tent at night in the shape of a yellow man (divine conception). When her older sons start to act suspiciously toward their late-arriving brothers, Alan stepped in to teach them an important lesson in survival. She gave them each a single arrow and commanded them to break it, which they easily did. Then she gave them five arrows tied together and commanded them to break the bundle, which of course none could do. The lesson is clear; after her death the brothers split up anyway but later reunited to raid and take captive a band of leaderless people camping together.

Recalling Mother Alan did little to soothe the resentment of Temüjin and Khasar. When Begter next took a bird away from his brothers, they snuck up on him seated on a hillock tending the horses and shot him at close range with their bows and arrows. Upon their return to the tent, Hö'elün immediately read the crime in their faces and poured out her wrath: ". . . citing old sayings, quoting ancient words, [she] mightily reviled her sons," accusing them of murder.

What does this episode explain to us, and more importantly, what was it supposed to teach Temüjin? We cannot doubt its veracity, or that Temüjin had a weightier motive to murder his stepbrother than the theft of a fish or a bird. It begins to make sense if we assume that Begter was a bit older than Temüjin and trying to assert prerogatives, which Temüjin disputed or found to be intolerable. Among those privileges, Begter may have been thinking of taking Yisügei's place as head of the family, according to the practice of levirate explained earlier. But as the elder son of the senior wife, Temüjin believed that he should assume leadership of the family. Among the Mongols, the principal of seniority mattered very much in such considerations. In the *Secret History*, Begter pleads with them to spare his younger brother Belgütei. They did, and Belgütei, chastened, became a firm and trusted supporter of Temüjin, who by some accounts later credited his world conquests to the strengths of his brothers Belgütei and Khasar. The relationship with Khasar, however, was not an easy one, as later events will show.

The murder of Begter sheds light on leadership and succession among the twelfth-century Mongols. An elder son did not automatically inherit his father's position, seniority notwithstanding. In parlous times, to be accepted as a leader you had to act like one. This meant defeating your rivals, by any means, and being generous and fair to your followers. Begter did not share the catch; he was presumptuous. Temüjin defeated him and showed generosity to Belgütei. For the first time, he asserted the qualities of a leader, one who did not take unnecessary risks and whom it would not do to cross. These traits were not always in harmony with other Mongol customs or the values his mother sought to instill. Yet a nomad's defining quality, if we can select but one, was his adaptability. Honor as adherence to fixed principles did not weigh in this mix.

Hö'elün's response suggests that she cherished all the children in her care, not merely the ones she gave birth to, and this is confirmed by her later penchant for raising children taken captive during her son's military career. Child mortality must have been high on the steppe, children were valued then as now, and Begter would have been contributing to the family's larder as an older son. The story highlights Hö'elün's role as an educator in key cultural values necessary for survival: family solidarity, cooperation, and loyalty. Here tensions surface between family survival and the ambitions of an emerging leader.

Temüjin perhaps learned these lessons: Strike while you can win (it does not matter how) and do not let others rob you of your patrimony. But take your mother's words to heart and foster the loyalty of your remaining brothers, for you will need it.

Temüjin's deed did not go unnoticed, leading, in the *Secret History*, to his capture and imprisonment by his Tayichi'ut relatives.

Friends

Perhaps fearing the youth's display of cunning, or wanting to check up on the boys he had abandoned years earlier, the Tayichi'ut chieftain Tarkhutai (Yisügei's cousin) rode into their encampment one day and demanded the surrender of the eldest son. Temüjin fled into a thicket for nine days (again the number nine!) before hunger drove him into his enemies' waiting arms. Borne off to the Tayichi'ut encampment, Temüjin was put in a cangue and passed around, spending one day under guard with each family. During a midsummer celebration, he eluded his keeper and lay low in a nearby stream. Soon enough a search was begun for the escapee. But the man who first spotted him, Sorkhan Shira, belonged to a subject clan of the Tayichi'ut and took pity on the boy, urging him to flee homeward. Instead, still hobbled and hungry, Temüjin returned under cover of darkness to Sorkhan's tent, where he had been treated well by Sorkhan's sons. The sons again welcomed Temüjin; destroyed the cangue; hid him in a cart of wool the next morning when the search was renewed; and sent him on his way with a horse, bow, and arrows.

Temüjin's knack for survival apparently stemmed from his keen ability to calculate timing and judge character. He probably reasoned that most people would get drunk during a celebration, making it a good time to slip away. (The Mongols were notorious tipplers and many future khans died of drinking.) Sorkhan Shira's subordinate status disposed him to help a victim of the Tayichi'ut. Clearly Temüjin also had a winning way with young people. In short, he was shrewd and charismatic, and he did not forget the favor shown him by Sorkhan Shira's family.

Temüjin tracked down his family and they moved their encampment to the banks of a stream in the hills south of the Mongols' sacred mountain Burkhan Khaldun, "where they stayed, killing marmots and field mice for food." One day a band of thieves made off with eight of the family's horses in broad daylight. A nomad's horses were his most prized possession, without which survival was both physically difficult and socially unbearable. Temüjin at once set off in pursuit riding the one remaining mount (nine horses!). Along the way he met a youth milking mares; the young man had seen the thieves passing by and promptly offered to help recover the stolen animals. Temüjin thus acquired his first *nökör*, or companion-in-arms, Bo'orchu, who took off without even informing his father, and returned days later only after they had retrieved the horses. Bo'orchu refused a share of the herd as a reward; his father, delighted to recover his son, had ample wealth and insisted that serving Temüjin was sufficient reward. Now joyful, the father urged the two young men "never to abandon each other!"; they never did.

Forging Alliances: The Bride

It was time for Temüjin, now about 16, to reclaim the most important ally of his life—his wife Börte. Belgütei accompanied him on the journey to Dei Sechen's encampment. At least six or eight years had elapsed since the two children had first met, and it was around the year 1180. Dei Sechen was relieved to find his son-in-law alive and gave his blessing to the marriage. After the celebration, Börte's parents saw the new couple off; her mother escorted the girl to Temüjin's camp, where Börte presented her mother-in-law with a black sable coat. This was no ordinary dowry, although garments often featured as a bride's present to her new in-laws. Black sable was an extraordinarily fine fur, and the long coat constituted a gift of immense value.

Married to a woman of a prominent lineage, newly confident at his recent successes, and determined to further improve his standing, Temüjin set about building a network of alliances and his own retinue of close followers, or *nököd*. First, he sent Belgütei to summon his new friend, Bo'orchu, who rode back with Belgütei, again without a word to his father. So far Temüjin could count on his brothers, especially Khasar, a keen archer, and Belgütei, whose enormous strength became legendary, and Bo'orchu. What he needed was a mentor or protector, someone older, more experienced, and more powerful. An obvious choice was his father's sworn friend or *anda,* Toghril khan of the Kereyit federation to their west. Furthermore, Temüjin must have known that his childhood *anda*, Jamukha, also served the Kereyit khan.

Toghril was a figure to be reckoned with in the uncertain political landscape of the northern steppes, albeit a troubled leader with blood on his hands. He was kidnapped at least twice in his childhood by enemy tribesmen, Merkit and Tatar, a fate that surely befalls a khan's son only with the connivance of his relatives. His lifelong struggles against them to secure the Kereyit throne tainted his reputation: He killed his Naiman stepbrothers after his father died; some of his brothers escaped his plots and plotted against him; his uncle dispossessed him, sending him into flight for seven or more years. The Persian historians disapprove of him. Yisügei, possibly against his elders' advice, rescued Toghril from his first exile and sent the posturing uncle packing to the Tangut realm, never to be seen again. (The Tanguts became infamous for harboring luckless steppe politicians, something they would pay for one day.) Following his father's example, Temüjin used Toghril as his own stepping stone and put Börte's gift to good use.

Toghril, or Ong-khan after the title he later earned from the Jurchen rulers of the Jin, was then camping west of the Mongols on the Tula River, near present-day Ulaanbaator. With Khasar and Belgütei at his side, Temüjin presented himself to Ong-khan and reminded the Kereyit leader that "since in earlier days you and my father declared yourselves sworn friends you are, indeed, like a father to me." Temüjin presented Börte's sable coat to his substitute father. Pleased with the offering and mindful of his obligations, Ong-khan promised to help Temüjin to reunite his "divided people." Doubtless he had other reasons to back the son of his *anda*; a strong Mongol leader could be of use to him, but perhaps not too strong. Temüjin's cousin and childhood *anda*, Jamukha, would see to that.

News of the alliance with Ong-khan spread, and Temüjin began to attract followers. A former subordinate of Yisügei brought his son Jelme, signifying acknowledgment of a transfer of authority from Yisügei to Temüjin. Jelme became one of Chinggis Khan's most celebrated warriors, one of the "four hounds" (with Khubilai, Jebe, and Sübetei). But unwanted visitors came calling as well. Early one morning a band of hostile Merkits approached Temüjin's camp. Everyone escaped on horseback except three women: Börte, Belgütei's mother, and an old serving woman who had sounded the alarm. Temüjin hid on Burkhan Khaldun until the Merkits departed with their female captives, having avenged Yisügei's earlier kidnapping of Hö'elün, the intended bride of one of their nobles. In keeping with the custom of levirate, they handed Börte over to the younger brother of Hö'elün's now-deceased fiancé.

Now, one might at first regard Temüjin's ignominious retreat as a mark of cowardice: Why didn't he grab Börte and carry her off to safety on his horse? Notions of European chivalry did not play on the medieval Mongol steppe. Chastity was an alien concept, impractical to nomads. (In China, a good woman would be expected to kill herself, to avoid this fate.) Women on the steppe were too valuable to slay and instead entered the victor's household, just as a woman would become the wife of her younger brother-in-law upon her husband's death. A man, however, ran the risk of getting killed if he stuck around to defend his family. Better to flee and return another day to take revenge and recapture lost loved ones. While some scholars see the *Secret History* story of Börte's abduction as literary invention, there is no doubt of her Merkit captivity, owing to the timing of her first pregnancy and uncertain paternity of the resulting child, which became an open source of friction among the adult sons of Chinggis Khan (as will become clear later in the story). The news of Temüjin reclaiming his bride (as well as allying with Ong-khan) no doubt reached Merkit ears, for any developments affecting the status of tribal feuds would be of great interest to all. The Merkits had a bone to pick with the Borjigins; now Temüjin had a bone to pick with the Merkits.

Moreover, the story we have serves two important functions. It introduces Temüjin's belief in his unique destiny and consequent devotion to the sacred mountain Burkhan Khaldun and the rituals associated with his worship of the mountain. He credited the mountain with saving his life, "a louse's life. Fearing for my life, my only life, I climbed the Khaldun . . .," and further admitted, "but I was greatly frightened. Every morning I will sacrifice to Burkhan Khaldun, every day I will pray to it. The offspring of my offspring shall be mindful of this and do likewise!" Temüjin thereupon took off his belt and draped it around his neck, in token of submission, "put his hat over his hand, beat his breast with his fist, and nine times kneeling down towards the sun, offered a libation and a prayer." Source of life, Burkhan Khaldun later became the resting ground for deceased members of the Golden Lineage.

The second narrative function of the Merkit raid is to provide Ong-khan with his cue for action. Temüjin did not take unnecessary risks. He turned to Ong-khan for help in responding to the Merkit raid and rescuing his bride. Having his own boyhood experience of Merkit captivity, Ong-khan readily agreed and enlisted the aid of his other young protégé, Jamukha, sworn friend of Temüjin. Jamukha too enters the narrative in the *Secret History* at this point to assume his fateful position in the triangular relationship that tied these men together in Temüjin's rise to power.

4

Making of a Khan,
1180s–1190s

Do not break this, your agreement; do not dissolve your bond, do not tear off your collar!

—THE SECRET HISTORY OF THE MONGOLS

The rescue of Börte was motivated by political as well as familial considerations and affords a glimpse into how twelfth-century nomads organized and deployed armies against one another. From the rescue of a woman the story shifts to the jostling for position as new leaders emerged on the Mongolian plateau. The stage enlarges as our sources begin to reveal how people from outside the Mongolian plateau became involved in the events unfolding there. Much remains uncertain in the sequence of events; the reconstruction offered in this chapter attempts to reconcile the often incomplete and contradictory accounts about these decades.

Family Matters

The Merkit campaign took place around 1182. In all likelihood, however, the campaign as described in the *Secret History* and other sources summarizes a series of Mongol operations against the Merkits over the space of several years in the early 1180s. Ong-khan laid out a battle plan, placing Jamukha in command: He himself would march forth with two units of ten thousand men each, forming the Right (i.e., western) Wing of the army; Jamukha would command another two units of ten thousand each to form the Left (i.e., eastern) Wing. Jamukha would decide when and where to rendezvous. Certainly the actual number of troops fielded was considerably smaller. Inner Asian military tradition, as practiced by the Kereyits, organized men into decimal units, of which the *tümen* or myriarchy (ten thousand) was the largest. We should understand these units as a measure of theoretical capability rather than as actual body count, and further as literary hyperbole, of which the *Secret History* and other sources furnish many such examples. Where would Jamukha, hardly older than Temüjin, find twenty thousand warriors? Probably Temüjin was supposed to contribute the other unit under Jamukha's command, but where would a Mongol teenager struggling to keep his family together raise ten thousand men at this point in his life? Nevertheless, Ong-khan's plan provides important evidence about twelfth-century military organization and practice on the Mongolian plateau. Chinggis Khan's later military reorganization adopted the Kereyit model illustrated here.

Temüjin sent Khasar and Belgütei to relay the plan to Jamukha; in this and similar instances the *Secret History* illustrates the value of verse in memorizing long messages for oral delivery. In the event, the forces of Ong-khan and Temüjin arrived at the rendezvous point specified by Jamukha, at the source of the Onon River in the Khentii Mountains, three days after Jamukha had arrived, and that was three days too late. Jamukha delivered a blistering greeting: "Did we not agree that we won't be late at the appointed meeting, even if there be a blizzard; at the gathering even if there be rain? Are we not Mongols, for whom a 'yes' is the same as being bound by an oath?" Ong-khan accepted the blame. But was this variation on the U.S. Postal Service's motto merely a lesson for the future khan from the friend who would not keep his own oath? Or a reminder to all subsequent reciters of the tale that timing is a critical factor in the planning and execution of a successful military operation? It has the ring of a later interpolation, a "memory" inserted into the "history" by a later group of Mongols for a specific reason.

The combined army moved north toward the forested southern shores of Lake Baikal and at nighttime fell upon the Merkit campgrounds on the banks of the Selenge River. As terrified Merkits scattered, trying to elude the plundering Mongols, Temüjin rode up and down the riverbank calling Börte's name. Fleeing in a cart with their old woman servant, she heard his voice, jumped down, and ran through the darkness toward him. "It was moonlight; he looked at them, recognized Lady Börte, and they fell into each other's arms." If not a complete invention, this reunion may have been the most, if not only, romantic moment in the future conqueror's life; as far as we can tell, he was not a sentimental man, allowed himself few weaknesses, and cherished ladies primarily as instruments of political alliance. (Later, as a khan and conqueror, he did indeed sire a large number of children from the steady stream of captured women entering his harem.) On the other hand, Temüjin was a lonely young man who needed his wife and no doubt cherished her and her loyalty to him.

The allies went no further; many Merkits and their chieftains escaped into the Siberian forests. The women and children left behind were taken as concubines or servants. Mother Hö'elün acquired her first orphan, a five-year old Merkit dressed in sable and skins. He and the other boys raised in Hö'elün's tent would grow up to assume command positions in the khan's army. Belgutei's mother did not turn up during this attack, and we hear no more about her.

Soon after her rescue, Börte gave birth to their eldest son, Jochi. The couple's second son, Chaghadai, born ca. 1186, resented his older brother and on one occasion called him (to his face) "this bastard offspring of the Merkit." Although both Temüjin and Börte knew that Jochi likely was fathered by her Merkit keeper, they never treated him other than as a proper elder son. Yet he was not his parents' favorite child and his descendants were never considered as candidates for succession to the office of Great Khan or *khaghan*, which complicated relations between the Golden Horde, Jochi's inheritance, and other territorial states in the Mongol Empire. Moreover, Jochi died before his father and was not buried on Burkhan Khaldun, the royal Chinggisid burial site. The name *Jochi* means "[unexpected] guest," perhaps a token of his special origins or his birth at Jamukha's camp. We know little about him, except that he liked to hunt and shoot, and was given to boasting, judging by Chaghadai's accusations. Jochi married a daughter of Jakha Gambu (Ong-khan's younger brother, evidently one who survived) and fathered Batu, later khan of the Golden Horde and the senior, most powerful Mongol behind the scenes in the 1230s and 1240s.

Rashid al-Din offers the pious fiction that Börte was pregnant before her capture by the Merkits. Polishing up the conqueror's past came naturally to Rashid, who loyally served a line of khans descended from Chinggis Khan's youngest son Tolui by another daughter of the Kereyit prince Jakha Gambu. Moreover, as a solidly patriarchal Persian, he probably could not comprehend such a careless attitude toward paternity.

By the time of Jochi's birth, and probably before her abduction, Börte and Temüjin may have already adopted a Tatar foundling, famous under the name *Shigi-Khutukhu*, who later served as recorder and judicial administrator of the early empire. The *Secret History* makes him out to be one of the orphans of Mother Hö'elün, raised as a brother to Temüjin. In Rashid al-Din's more plausible account, teenaged Temüjin picked up Shigi-Khutukhu in an early battle with the Tatars and sent him to the as-yet childless Börte. Having her own male child to rear would give Börte a certain position in the family, that is, in relation to her influential mother-in-law, Hö'elün, with whom she no doubt spent almost all of her time. The foundling's attachment to the family and his subsequent prestige emerge through his youthful service to and affectionate regard for his adoptive parents, his grief at Börte's funeral, and his long and distinguished career. Being adopted, he would of course not figure in the ranks of candidates to succeed Chinggis Khan.

Tribal Relations

The Merkit campaign marked Temüjin's first military success, in concert with his new allies Ong-khan and Jamukha. Ong-khan returned to his base camp on the Tula River. Jamukha meanwhile invited Temüjin to renew their old friendship and remain with him, sharing his camp. Exchanging golden belts and horses looted from the Merkit chieftains, "they declared themselves sworn friends and loved each other; they enjoyed themselves revelling and feasting, and at night they slept together, the two of them alone under their blanket." This was no homophilic affiliation; the reader should not interpret Börte's later part in breaking up the partnership as a sign of sexual jealousy. A split was inevitable between two such ambitious and charismatic young men competing for leadership over the Mongols. Temüjin's troublesome Tayichi'ut relatives also numbered among Jamukha's followers.

One day about a year and a half later, Jamukha's combined band packed up and set out for their summer campgrounds. As the two sworn friends rode along together up front, Jamukha made a puzzling suggestion about where they should pitch camp that evening. Unsure of his intent, Temüjin dropped back to seek his mother's advice. Traveling with Hö'elün, Börte broke in to say that Jamukha had obviously grown tired of them and they ought to move on and camp separately from him. Everyone agreed. Temüjin's party continued on through the night, collecting another little boy for Hö'elün as they passed the Tayichi'ut camp. Not surprisingly, the Tayichi'ut opted to side with Jamukha in the breakup. Other kinfolk decamped to follow Temüjin, whose swelling ranks assembled their tents at Temüjin's old home on Blue Lake near the Black Heart Mountain south of Burkhan Khaldun. Interestingly, the old family retainer Mönglik (called Father Mönglik) elected to stay with Jamukha.

Scholars have proposed theories of social class tensions to explain the rivalry between the two young Mongol chiefs, and the motives behind Jamukha's riddle proposing two camp locations, mountain or river, each of which presented practical problems for a nomad. Yet both young men were "upper-class" Mongols of good lineage; Jamukha was a chief or prince among the Jadaran, and Temüjin's father had likewise been a prominent chief of his Borjigin sublineage. Jamukha has been cast as representing the claims of established tribal aristocrats or lineage elders (the "princes") to leadership over everyone else, including juniors like Temüjin. By having Börte interpret Jamukha's words as hostile, did the *Secret History* editors try to shift any blame for abandoning Jamukha away from its hero? Perhaps Börte thought that ambiguous words hide treachery: A true friend or ally speaks directly and makes his or her meaning clear. The family may have grown tired of Jamukha. Whatever actually passed between them, Temüjin's party found a pretext to make a bid for autonomy in line with his own desire for self-mastery, a desire fully anticipated and promoted by Börte. Further impetus may have come, inadvertently, from Temüjin's clan elders, Altan, Kuchar, and Sacha-beki, who also departed Jamukha's camp and made their way to Blue Lake to throw their support behind Temüjin.

Around the time of the parting of the sworn friends, Börte gave birth to their second son, Chaghadai, the future ruler of central Asia.

Election as Khan

Some time after the realignment of forces, Temüjin's allies elected him as their khan on the shores of Blue Lake at Black Heart Mountain. Senior clansmen Altan, Kuchar, and Sacha-beki (the Jurkin leader) renounced their own eligibility for Borjigin leadership and pledged allegiance to the young Temüjin, perhaps imagining that they could mold him to their own purposes. When Jamukha received news of the election, according to the *Secret History*, he returned this message: "Why did you, Altan and Kuchar, cause a split between sworn friend Temüjin and myself? . . . why did you not make sworn friend Temüjin khan when we were still together . . .? You, Altan and Kuchar, keep to the words you have spoken . . . be the good companions of my sworn friend!"

Jamukha appeared to divert the blame for any misunderstanding or disloyalty onto others, whom he urged to be steady in their service (of course they would not be steady, justifying their later elimination). To Temüjin's messengers the

Kereyit khan (overlord of both Temüjin and Jamukha) replied, "To make my son Temüjin khan is indeed right. How can the Mongols be without a khan?" Ong-khan appeared confident that the new Mongol khan would continue to serve him as a loyal son and perhaps trim Jamukha's sails. He too urged Temüjin's officers to show their new master the same faith. Faith, loyalty, and betrayal: The saga recounted in the *Secret History* takes every opportunity to lecture on these virtues and portray Temüjin as faithful and generous, and others as disloyal, petty, or cruel.

The year of this first election is uncertain, sometime between 1184 and 1189. Although the *Secret History* refers to him from then on as Chinggis Kha'an (i.e., not merely khan, but *khan of khans)*, this is a pretty clear case of anachronism. The weight of informed opinion favors Temüjin receiving the title by which the world knows him at the 1206 *khuriltai*, or assembly, which elected him khan over all the tribes on the Mongolian plateau. This early local affair, which merely promoted his candidacy for that position, involved mainly his immediate kin and close friends. At this juncture, he was no older than 28.

The new khan's first acts were organizational and showed a certain serious-ness of purpose. As befitted a rising leader, he set up a household staff, and from the ranks of allies, new and old, appointed cooks, quiver bearers, stewards, herders, wagoners, guards, and equerries or attendants in charge of the royal mounts. His closest companions (not his brothers), Bo'orchu and Jelme, super-vised the household establishment. The new organization gradually expanded into a royal bodyguard (*keshig*), which assumed both civil and military functions as the core of the imperial administration that emerged in the early thirteenth century.

Jamukha's Pique

Sometime after Temüjin's elevation, but probably no later than 1190, friction between the former friends bubbled over into open conflict sparked by horse theft. Although the *Secret History* tries to blame one of Jamukha's dependents, the two sides engaged in mutual provocation. Temüjin's partisans took the usual recourse: Pursue the thief, kill him, and reclaim the horses. Jamukha retaliated in force. A pitched battle between armies assembled by the two leaders ensued in the Kerulen basin near the Onon River. Jamukha's troops smashed Temüjin's forces and sent him into retreat. Evidently out of sheer spite, Jamukha then had some of his higher-ranking captives boiled alive in cauldrons, which suggests ritual sacrifice of an enemy, a gruesome detail possibly invented to discredit him. He also cut off the head of a defeated chieftain and dragged it around tied to his horse's tail.

The Mongols shared a taboo against shedding blood, which they believed to house the human soul. If possible, one should kill without splattering a lot of gore about, thus redirecting the potency of the deceased spirit to serve oneself. Custom decreed that honorable adversaries be executed by suffocation through one means or another, although custom did not always hold sway. News of Jamukha's horrific excesses spread like wildfire and appear in all of our sources, testifying to a general revulsion against his treatment of opponents. A number of Jamukha's followers, including Yisüge's retainer, Father Mönglik, and his seven sons, deserted to Temüjin's side. Things began to look up again for the young Mongol chief. Jamukha thereafter pursued a campaign of courting potential opposition to his rival that occupied him to his dying day.

At some point in the early 1190s, Temüjin and his Jurkin relatives hosted a celebratory feast on the banks of the Onon. The event turned riotous. A beverage server violated protocol by pouring koumiss, the Mongols' customary tipple made from fermented mare's milk, for a junior Jurkin wife ahead of two senior ladies. A Jurkin stole a horse tether, and the two stewards, Belgütei, on the Kiyad Borjigin side, and Büri Bökö (the Wrestler, a cousin of Yisügei), on the Jurkin Borjigin side, fell to grappling in the time-honored way of settling disputes. Belgütei lost to Büri, the wrestling champion of his people. Temüjin and the others, perhaps drunk, ignored Belgütei's pleas to keep the peace with the Jurkins. A brawl erupted, breaking up the party. Later peace feelers passed to and fro, seeking to patch over the quarrel among these Mongols.

Although the Jurkins had spearheaded Temüjin's election as khan, their conduct in this episode makes clear that they were keeping their options open and possibly did not take him too seriously as a contender for supreme power. Their backsliding may have stiffened Temüjin's resolve to get revenge, when it became possible. It may also have convinced him to shun inebriating beverages, or strictly moderate his use of them. You cannot be both drunk and in control at the same time. Unlike many of his drink-loving descendants, Temüjin comes down to us a sober man, but this anecdote in the *Secret History* shows him losing his temper and ignoring the advice of his stepbrother and staunch friend. Though he attributed his survival to the favor of Tengri (Heaven's destiny), claimed as the singular birthright of Temüjin and his lineage, sobriety undoubtedly reinforced it.

When Temüjin called upon his Jurkin relations to support his campaign against the Tatars in 1196, they ignored him, to their own undoing.

The Kereyit Khan and the Tatar Campaign

The Tatar campaign of 1196, unlike the rest of the 1180s and 1190s, is dated reliably in Chinese accounts. The silence of our sources otherwise for these decades suggests a time of continued struggle and humiliating reversals, such as the one the Onon banquet episode hints at. Some scholars have proposed that Temüjin underwent a period of exile in Jurchen territory to the south, something that might have been suppressed in the record of the great world conqueror's rise to power. One southern Chinese diplomat's account of a 1221 embassy to Jurchen-ruled north China even claims that Temüjin spent ten years in servitude to the Jin. An extended residence along the Jin frontier would have doubled his determination to unite the Mongols and attack the Jin, to requite the many insults suffered at Jurchen hands. Arguably, though, the Chinese envoy heard a garbled tale about Kereyit princely turmoil and exile in the southwest. Such rumors circulated around north China in the late twelfth century.

One difficulty lies in dating the volatile career of Kereyit leader Ong-khan. He had once more lost his throne to a discontented brother (who, possibly with another sibling, Jakha Gambu, earlier had taken refuge among the Naiman) and had to flee again to the Qara Khitai realm in central Asia, passing through Tangut and Uighur settlements. For a while, his Naiman-supported sibling ruled the Kereyits. Ong-khan made his way back to Mongolia and took shelter with Temüjin, who helped him to regain his position; in this act, self-interest coincided neatly with duty to his sworn father. Though something has surely been omitted in the record, we will assume that Ong-khan was in Mongolia for the Tatar campaign.

Early in the summer of 1196, Temüjin and Ong-khan campaigned against the Tatars on behalf of the Jurchen emperor or the Altan Khan ("Golden Khan"; Jin, the Chinese name of the Jurchen dynasty, means "gold"). For decades the Tatars had been assisting the Jin rulers to restrain unruly tribes such as the Mongols, but periodically they turned in resentment against their overlords and raided the border, as happened in the 1190s. The Jurchens now invited the Mongols and other enemies of the Tatars to attack the latter. A Jin commander drove the rebellious tribes into Mongol territory, where Temüjin and Ong-khan assaulted, looted, and dispersed a band of their old foes, killing its leader. They then reported to the Jurchen general's camp to collect the promised reward.

For his part, Temüjin received a middling title of uncertain meaning, possibly of Khitan origin. The *Secret History* claims that the Kereyit khan received the title "ong" (from *wang*, Chinese for "prince") at the same time, but Toghril's exploit seems insufficiently grand for that return; the relatively exalted though purely honorary title of *wang* would have come directly from the Jin emperor and probably for some other reason. Interestingly, in the *Secret History* the Jin commander states that he would ask the Altan Khan if Temüjin did not deserve a loftier title. Possibly the Jin court granted the aging Kereyit chieftain his lofty title later that year or soon after, to stiffen his unsteady authority and play off Temüjin against him. It was standard frontier policy to keep the nomads weak and divided. Nevertheless, by the late 1190s Ong-khan was in Temüjin's debt, and never allowed to forget it. Though Temüjin still needed Ong-khan, the elderly Kereyit lacked the means to challenge his ambitions; hounded by family tensions and a jealous son, Ong-khan found himself torn between an unstable throne and a talented and tenacious junior khan.

Though the Tatar victory marked a turning point in the relationship between Temüjin and Ong-khan, its deeper significance pointed to the south, where lay wealth. With it an aspiring khan could attract and keep adherents, for a free nomad's main reason for following a leader was the promise of regular booty, the steppe equivalent of salary. It would be a long time yet before campaigning beyond Mongolia figured into this khan's calculations, but everyone knew that China offered the best booty, and revenge was a powerful motivator. In the Tatar plunder acquired by Temüjin figured the vanquished chieftain's silver cradle and a quilt embroidered with pearls, no doubt products of China gifted by the Jin court to the Tatar leaders. One wonders if the glittering loot interested Temüjin more than the title, for the title put Temüjin in a vassal relationship with

the Jin court and obliged him to pay annual "tribute" to the Jurchens. This obligation renewed the unsatisfactory situation that the Mongols found themselves in
vis-à-vis the Jin in the 1160s. Rather than succeeding or emulating the Tatars in
their relationship with the Jin dynasty, the Mongol chief almost certainly
intended to become his own overlord and distribute such luxuries in lavish dis-
plays of generosity to loyal subjects, as a good khan should.

In the Tatar battle, the *Secret History* tells us that Temüjin and Ong-khan
"shared the booty, each taking his part; then they returned to their own encampments." Sharing was the customary practice. Though technically still the junior
vassal, Temüjin expected Ong-khan to coordinate all booty-taking activities with
him, and when the Kereyit did not do so, he chafed. Temüjin subsequently insti-
tuted a new policy regarding loot seized in battle. First, however, he had to deal
with his Jurkin relatives, whose failure to support the coalition against their ancient
Tatar enemies provided justification for ridding himself of some potential rivals.

Disciplining the Borjigins

The Jurkins had agreed to join the anti-Tatar alliance but failed to show up after
six days. Adding insult to injury, they raided Temüjin's home camp while he was
off fighting, stripping the clothes from fifty men and killing ten. Whether a fabri-
cation by later chroniclers to justify their punishment or a measure of Jurkin
political ineptitude (or poverty), the incident enraged the Mongol khan. He set
forth, this time without Kereyit support (perhaps Ong-khan was on his way into
exile again). Temüjin attacked their camp, chasing down his elder cousin Sacha-
beki and Sacha's son, who confessed that they had not kept the oath of loyalty
sworn when they elected him their leader. The khan had them beheaded and
abandoned their bodies. No suffocation or ritual burial for perfidy and betrayal
of one's khan! Exit two senior kinsmen, the last eligible candidates for Borjigin
leadership (not counting Yisügei's still faithful younger brother, Temüjin's uncle
Daritai).

The remaining Jurkins, including Büri, the wrestler, entered the victors' households and service as subject people. Wary of the man who had so affronted
Belgütei at the Onon feast, Temüjin proposed a wrestling match between them,
knowing full well that Büri could throw his stepbrother. Büri knew it too, but no
longer dared. He let Belgütei topple him and straddle his back. At a signal from
his brother, Belgütei proceeded to snap the wrester's spine. Thus the khan satisfied his desire for revenge without danger of retribution. It seems a cowardly
deed, unrecorded in other sources. Why, then, does the *Secret History* preserve it?
The Mongol epic, remember, is more than (and sometimes quite less than) an
exaltation of Chinggis Khan; it recounts the genealogies of the Mongol clans, cel-
ebrates their virtues, and sympathizes with their struggles. The Jurkins, also
Borjigins, were a proud people "gall in their livers, thumbs good at shooting,
lungs filled with courage, mouths full of fury, and, all, men of skill." Büri was a
great athlete who died an honorable death (no blood was shed), unlike the Jurkin
elders.

These events probably took place sometime in the winter of 1196–1197. It took Temüjin almost ten more years to eliminate his rivals and win over or suppress their followers to become master of the Mongolian plateau. Through this struggle, a new sociopolitical formation began taking shape on the plateau as defeated tribespeople and their surviving leaders were either incorporated into the Mongol khan's growing federation or escaped southward, followed in time by pursuing Mongol troops.

CHAPTER

5

Uniting the People, 1197–1205

I have no other face than that known to the Khan.

—THE SECRET HISTORY OF THE MONGOLS

From the final critical years of Chinggis Khan's rise to power on, we begin to have more and better documentation on which to rest our tale. It turns, at this point, on the precarious relationship between the Mongol chief and his Kereyit backers. Ong-khan's vacillation and his son Ilkha Senggüm's resistance eventually brought a showdown between the allies. The older khan wielded less and less authority and his son more and more, and we should probably see in the Kereyit chief's apparent acts of betrayal the hand of his unhappy heir. Once it became clear that Temüjin had prevailed over the Kereyits by supplanting their leadership, the tribal opposition to him collapsed. Yet nothing about his success was inevitable; at any point he could have been killed and the course of Eurasian (and world) history would have carved out a different channel.

Uneasy Alliances

In 1197, Temüjin presented Ong-khan with the loot from a joint Mongol–Kereyit raid on the Merkits, to help the senior khan rally his supporters and to demonstrate continued loyalty to his sworn father. Thus fortified, in 1198 Ong-khan attacked the Merkits on his own, keeping the spoils of his raid, to Temüjin's annoyance. Although the *Secret History* narrative emphasizes a settling of debts of vengeance, the dynamics between Temüjin and Ong-khan meant that their every action now assumed an additional political meaning. Their "dual kingship" was inherently unstable.

Temüjin's irritation did not stop a Mongol–Kereyit attack in 1199 on the powerful Naimans, the Kereyits' western enemies, whose feuding leadership had split the Naiman federation between two brothers: Buyirukh khan, on northern slopes of the Altai Mountains, and Tayang khan of the steppes around the Irtysh River. Buyirukh fared badly and beat a retreat to safety. Returning eastward, the allies met a contingent of Tayang khan's soldiers belatedly sent to repulse them, but as it was nightfall, they all pitched camp to resume battle the following morning, as custom decreed. According to the *Secret History*, Jamukha persuaded Ong-khan to sneak away under cover of darkness, leaving his sworn son to face the Naimans alone. Naiman forces instead pursued the withdrawing Kereyit, capturing Ilkha Senggüm's family and followers, as well as Ong-khan's baggage and cattle; Jamukha escaped. Helpless, Ong-khan appealed yet again to Temüjin, who kept the peace between them by sending his four best warriors to recover Ong-khan's properties. The Kereyit attempt (Senggüm's brainchild? or Jamukha's?) to get rid of the Mongol khan thus backfired.

Temüjin put up with the perfidious Kereyit in order to neutralize Jamukha and take the place of Ong-khan's heir, Senggüm, whom the *Secret History* and Rashid al-Din portray as Jamukha's dupe, gullible, and aggrieved. It is not hard to understand Senggüm's resentment of his father's adoptive son, or his numerous plots against Temüjin, yet all attempts to unseat his rival failed. Obviously Heaven (Tengri) did not favor Senggüm, or the other tribal elites.

In 1200 Temüjin met with Ong-khan near his camp on the Tula River to discuss their future and reaffirm their relationship. Rashid al-Din adds that at this gathering another plot to slay Temüjin was foiled and did not derail a successful Mongol–Kereyit assault on the Tayichi'uts, along the Onon banks. Recall that the Tayichi'uts had kidnapped the Mongol khan in his youth, and now Temüjin exacted vengeance. Several Tayichi'ut princes perished and the captured women and children were distributed among Temüjin's officers. Those who escaped enjoyed only a short reprieve.

News of Temüjin's victories over the Naimans and Tayichi'uts spread rapidly and galvanized hostile or unaligned tribal elites into action. Fearful of losing their independence and traditional status through absorption into the Mongol organization, chiefs of lesser tribes (the Oirats, farther west), dissident Mongols (the Jadaran, Jamukha's clan), and survivors of earlier battles (Tatars, Merkits, Naimans, Tayichi'uts) gathered on the Argun River in 1201 to swear allegiance over the sacrifice of a stallion and a mare, and to name Jamukha their *gür khan* (universal khan). Hö'elün's tribe, the Onggirat, came to join the Mongol camp, but Temüjin's brother Khasar misread their intentions and despoiled them, sending them off to unite with the opposition coalescing around Jamukha.

The anti-Mongol alliance then set out to attack Temüjin and his Kereyit allies. Forewarned of their intention, Temüjin sent for Ong-khan to advance against the foe. They joined battle at Köyiten (between the Onon and Kerulen rivers), one of the most critical confrontations of Temüjin's life. Soon after the armies clashed, the Naiman Buyirukh khan and an Oirat chieftain conjured up a magical snowstorm to blind and bewilder their opponents, but instead "the magic storm rolled back and it was right upon themselves that it fell. Unable to proceed, they tumbled into ravines. Saying to one another, 'We are not loved by Heaven!' they scattered." No doubt this supernatural miscarriage masks hard and bloody combat, but the outcome seems clear. Jamukha arrived late and quickly retreated; pursued by Ong-khan, he plundered some of his defeated friends on the way back to his own territory. Temüjin took off after the retreating Tayichi'uts, his personal enemies, and engaged them decisively in a battle that nearly took his life.

The Tayichi'ut and Tatar Campaigns

At nightfall on the first day, the opposing sides set up camps right where they had fought along the banks of the Onon. Temüjin had taken an arrow in his neck and was bleeding profusely. Frantic that he could not stop the blood flow, he submitted to the care of his *nökör*, Jelme, who kept sucking the blood from the wound and spitting it out, even after it had started to coagulate. Jelme realized that the arrow was poisoned and that only by keeping the blood flowing could he wash out the poison and reduce the likelihood of death.

To quench the reviving khan's thirst, in the middle of the night Jelme snuck into the enemy camp, "stark naked but for his pants," to steal provisions, but could find only a bucket of curds. To this he added some water and fed Temüjin. The next morning, Temüjin noticed the bloody puddles around him and remarked ungratefully, "What is this? Couldn't you have spat further away?" Jelme pointed out that he had had to swallow a great deal as well, a notable sacrifice given the Mongols' taboos against the spilling of blood (and against choking). Related only in the *Secret History*, the story has the ring of myth. Jelme explains that he shed his clothes before entering the enemy camp in order to provide himself with an excuse should he be caught: He could claim to be defecting to the Tayichi'uts after being stripped by suspicious Mongols. Jelme, one of the feared "four hounds" of Temüjin, earned great honor for his meritorious service during the distribution of rewards at the 1206 assembly.

Recovered from his wound, Temüjin spent the next day tracking down fugitives, among them the friendly family that had helped him escape his boyhood captivity in the Tayichi'ut encampment. He spared these folks, along with an honest (or boastful) subordinate clansman who had shot an arrow into the neck of Temüjin's favorite horse at Köyiten. Admiring the man's ready admission of his deed, Temüjin renamed him Jebe (arrow) and made him one of his close companions. Rashid al-Din records a less heroic version of Jebe's surrender to Temüjin, but however it happened, Jebe became the first of his "four hounds" and a superb general.

Temüjin had a knack for picking his men. Honesty and loyalty ranked high; if a man, no matter how talented, betrayed his rightful master to Temüjin, the latter treated it as treason and usually had the offender put to death. Many stories in the *Secret History* play on this theme. Some Tayichi'ut refugees who made their way to Temüjin's camp confessed that they had intended to turn over their fugitive chieftain, caught hiding in the woods, but let him go upon recalling the likely consequences. Temüjin confirmed their decision: "Your feeling that you should not betray your lawful master was correct." These stories probably do not tell us what actually happened; rather they convey important moral and political lessons, which were equally or more significant to the Mongols who recorded and retold them.

As for the rest of the defeated foe, Temüjin "wiped out the men of the Tayichi'ut lineage.... he blew them to the winds like hearth ashes, even to the offspring of their offspring," in the epic hyperbole of the *Secret History*, and absorbed the women and children into his growing organization. Then he set his sights on the Tatars. Why not avenge his father, Yisügei, and better still, rid the steppe of one more obstacle to his rule over all the tribes of eastern Mongolia? The Kereyits, though disorganized, could still muster considerable resources. The time to take control of them had not yet arrived.

Traditional masters of the high eastern steppe for centuries, the Tatars far out-stripped the Mongols in manpower, wealth, and cultural prestige, owing to their contacts with the rich southern civilization. From the winter of 1201 through the spring of 1202, the Mongol camp made preparations for the Tatar campaign. While his troops rested, Temüjin and his top generals conferred and issued a new code of battle discipline:

> If we overcome the enemy, we shall not stop for booty. When the victory is com-plete, that booty will surely be ours, and we will share it among ourselves. If we are forced by the enemy to retreat, let us turn back to the point where we began the attack. Those men who do not turn back to the point where we began the attack shall be cut down!

This represented a break from past practice in which nomads fought largely in exchange for the right to take booty; that is, chieftains distributed the spoils of war among their own followers, after rendering their khan his due. With this order, Temüjin claimed the authority to take all the booty and redistribute it as he deemed proper. He anticipated some resistance from his chief officers to the new order in the upcoming Tatar campaign, especially from the warriors of aristo-cratic lineage.

In the autumn of 1202 the Mongol coalition overwhelmed and routed the Tatar federation in the hills south of the Khalkha River. Sure enough, three senior men of Temüjin's own clan, two brothers and a cousin of Yisügei, defied the decree and "stopped for booty," forcing Temüjin to relieve them of their pickings. Not sur-prisingly, the disgruntled princes departed to the camp of Ong-khan, who did not participate in this Tatar campaign. After the initial victory, Temüjin conferred with his inner circle about the disposition of the defeated enemy and decided to elimi-nate most of the adults and enslave the rest. Or, as Temüjin's stepbrother Belgütei explained unwisely to a curious Tatar waiting outside the tent, "We have decided to measure you all against the linchpin of a cart and slay you." The prisoner immediately bolted and, urging his comrades to barricade themselves against the Mongols and fight to the last man, provoked a bloody coda to their battlefield loss. Belgütei's indiscretion got him barred from further inner councils.

The Tatar victory also brought Temüjin two new wives (daughters of the curi-ous Tatar mentioned earlier), the sisters Yisüi and Yisügen, who became favorites among the growing ranks of his consorts. Yisüi was appointed a consort of the second rank and first or principal wife of the third *ordo*, or "palace encampment," over which each principal wife presided. Yisügen, the younger, headed the wives belonging to the fourth *ordo*. According to Rashid al-Din, Chinggis had nearly five hundred wives and concubines (perhaps an exaggeration) of which five ranked as grand ladies with an *ordo*, including the Tatar sisters. Lady Börte, number one wife, presided over her own *ordo* at the top of the hierarchy. Elite Mongols practiced polygamy as a form of diplomacy and politics. The Mongol khan's progress can be measured by the women who entered his household and reigned over an *ordo* establishment, each with its own treasury of wealth to dispense, subject peoples, and often troops. Having plucked two Tatar princesses, Temüjin turned to harvest the Kereyits.

Assuming the Kereyit Throne

Ong-khan sat out the Tatar battle, nursing his domestic woes and dreading the future. The political landscape of the steppe was shifting inexorably against him. In 1203 he considered reconciliation with Temüjin. The Mongols had proposed a marriage alliance, an exchange of daughters: Ong-khan's daughter (Senggüm's sister) to Temüjin's eldest son, Jochi; a daughter of Temüjin for a son of Senggüm. The proposal outraged Senggüm, whose loathing for the Mongol chief only inflated his own sense of superiority and fear of losing the Kereyit throne. Jamukha and other dissident steppe leaders, fearful as well, sided with Senggüm and tried to convince Ong-khan that Temüjin was communicating treacherously with the Naimans, the traditional brokers of power among contending Kereyit princes.

Ong-khan did not trust Jamukha, but his obligation to Temüjin did not outweigh his attachment to his own son; he feared his son's alienation more than Temüjin. Marco Polo's account of the breach attributes the wrath excited by Temüjin's marriage proposal to Ong-khan (whom he calls Prester John) rather than to Senggüm: "What impudence is this, to ask for my daughter's hand in marriage! Does he not know well that I am his liege and he my vassal? Go back and tell him that I would sooner set my daughter in the fire than give her in marriage to him, and that he deserves death at my hand, rebel and traitor that he is!" But Ong-khan could not stomach an open confrontation, so he finally agreed to a scheme hatched by Senggüm to lure Temüjin to a betrothal feast and kill him there. Pleased at the Kereyit invitation, Temüjin set out unsuspecting in the spring of 1203 accompanied only by several companions. While camping along the way with his old family retainer, Father Mönglik, he got wind of the plot against him and fled into hiding, sending two men on in his stead. Their arrival without Temüjin signaled that the Kereyit plan had backfired, and the hosts set out instead to chase down and capture their Mongol nemesis. News of this also leaked, conveniently, to the Mongol khan.

Temüjin headed southeast with a few trusty men and no baggage, to the Khalakhaljit Sands. After recruiting some deserters from Jamukha's camp, he met the Kereyit attack. Though Senggüm suffered a face wound, the Mongols took heavy losses and retreated further into a marshy area south of the Khalkha River, at a bracken river or lake called Baljuna, in southeast Mongolia near the Jin frontier. Greatly reduced in numbers and lacking provisions, the survivors held out and awaited reinforcements. Some missing comrades rejoined them and together, some nineteen leaders (not the rank-and-file nomad soldiery), they drank the bitter Baljuna water and swore an oath, to seal their alliance against the Kereyits. According to a Chinese record of this event, Temüjin vowed, "When I have completed this great task I will share the bitter and sweet fruits with you. If I break my word, may I become like the Baljuna waters." Despite the optimism of these words, at this point Tengri seemed to have abandoned Temüjin.

Scholars have debated whether the swearing of a covenant at Baljuna actually took place, and if so, when it happened and who participated in it. Although not described in the *Secret History*, other sources confirm that survivors of the battle, among them Khitans, Tanguts, Muslims, and even some Kereyit allies of the Mongols, swore an oath to signal their common purpose in toppling Ong-khan's dynasty. Later biographies of these warriors always refer to their status as *Baljuna men*, a badge of high honor.

As the months wore on, Temüjin's armies regrouped themselves for the final showdown, while the Kereyits, oblivious to the threat, celebrated their victory over the Mongols. A Muslim trader named Asan from Önggüt territory to the south along the Jin border passed by with his caravan to water his animals. Asan endeared himself to the Mongol chief by supplying mutton to the hungry refugees. He may have been the same merchant, Hasan Hajji, who loyally served Chinggis Khan during his central Asian campaign some fifteen years later.

In the summer of 1203 Temüjin and his followers left Baljuna and made their way back to his base camp between the Kerulen and Onon rivers. There the Mongol chieftain dispatched envoys in all directions, delivering oral exhortations to Ong-khan, Jamukha, Senggüm, his relatives, Börte's relatives, and other former adherents. New recruits and older allies who had sided with Ong-khan gathered to swell the Mongol ranks, which by now counted members of all the tribal groups on the Mongolian plateau. Their horses fattened from summer grazing, the replenished Mongol forces gathered on the Onon River for an autumn attack on the Kereyits.

The return of his estranged brother Khasar further bolstered Temüjin's confidence. Tensions between the two brothers had apparently led to Khasar's voluntary withdrawal to a separate campground sometime earlier. Persian and Chinese sources explain that in 1203 Khasar's family was living at Ong-khan's camp, taken captive in a Kereyit raid from which Khasar and one son escaped and went looking for Temüjin. This circumstance provided the Mongol khan a ruse. Envoys traveled to the Kereyit camp to deliver a message from Khasar, promising that he would join Ong-khan if the Kereyits sent him a trusted messenger. That unfortunate man walked into a Mongol trap.

Temüjin proceeded with his usual caution and deception, taking Ong-khan by surprise; this suggests that the Kereyits' combined forces still exceeded Mongol manpower. The Mongols surrounded the Kereyit khan's camp and battled for several days. Ong-khan fled at night and was killed by a Naiman patrol, who doubted their disheveled captive's claim to be the Kereyit khan. Senggüm escaped south to the Tangut lands and from there was chased into central Asia, where he was later tracked down and executed. Temüjin distributed the surviving Kereyits among his top warriors. He spared Jakha Gambu, Ong-khan's younger brother, and gave Sorkhakhtani-beki, one of Jakha Gambu's daughters, to his youngest son Tolui in marriage, while taking the elder daughter, Ibakha-beki, for himself. Later, in 1206, he awarded Ibakha to one of his trusted commanders who had fought off Kereyit troops at the Khalakhaljit Sands, wounded Senggüm, and then hunted down and executed the girl's father, who had begun plotting against his new Mongol overlord. Ibakha's dowry included 200 servants (further evidence of Kereyit affluence and status) of which the Mongol khan asked to keep 100 "to remember you" by.

Endgame: Jamukha and the Naimans

Foreseeing Ong-khan's demise and unwilling to recognize Temüjin as the new Kereyit khan, Jamukha and Temüjin's clan elders Altan, Daritai, and Kuchar (perhaps Jakha Gambu with them) had earlier deserted to the Naimans. Temüjin's old Merkit foe, Toghto'a-beki, also numbered among those who remained outside the Mongol federation.

Among the Naimans, power lay in the hands of Khan Tayang's levirate wife, Gürbesü Khatun (his stepmother; some accounts cite this as the source of the quarrel between the two brothers of the late khan). The *Secret History* offers a pungent description of her, and the entire Naiman episode was clearly embroidered with an eye to entertaining its audience. Being older and more experienced, as well as a strong woman of pronounced views, the energetic Khatun despised her diffident stepson and ridiculed the Mongols: "The Mongol people have always smelled bad and worn grimy clothes. They live far apart, and far away. Let them stay there. But we might perhaps have their fine daughters and daughters-in-law brought here and, making them wash their hands, perhaps just let them milk our cows and sheep." She dispatched messengers to the Önggüt Turks living south of the Gobi, offering an alliance to "take the quivers of those few Mongols!"

Despite being Nestorian Christian and Turk, like the Naimans, the Önggüt chief Alakhush Digit Khuri was on friendly terms with Temüjin. His envoy found Temüjin hunting on the steppes north of the Onon River and delivered the warning that the Naiman khan "is coming to take your quivers." After some discussion with his men, many of whom wanted to postpone battle until the horses had fattened up some more, Temüjin set about reorganizing his army to prepare for battle against the Naiman coalition.

Up to that time, the fighting manpower that the Mongols relied on had been comprised mainly of separate clan chieftains, often of uncertain loyalty, each commanding his own group of followers, that is, those warriors attached personally to him through ties of kinship, servitude, or voluntary association (*anda*-ship). A khan did not have direct control over all of these men, the rank-and-file steppe soldiery. At any time chieftains might stay home, or followers absond to another chieftain. Around that time, Temüjin began to implement changes, which dramatically altered the shape and dynamics of his army for the next several years, creating a more effective and pliable instrument of war. He divided his men decimally into groups of thousands (chiliarchies), hundreds (under the thousands), and tens (under the hundreds); and to each group appointed a commander. Thus he brought his troop organization into line with the steppe tradition of decimal organization and with the Kereyit army, which

Ong-khan had organized into groups of ten thousand (*tümen,* myriarchies) decades earlier.

The fact that Temüjin had not yet set up myriarchies (ten thousands) indicates that his army remained small in comparison with the Kereyit military at its height, and even with contemporary Naiman forces, which now led the remaining tribal opposition. At that time Temüjin also reorganized his personal bodyguards, designating six chamberlains, who, as before, had responsibility for his household and property. The Mongol khan further set up a day guard of seventy men and a night guard of eighty men, along with a special unit to stand arrayed before him during time of battle. The guards, *keshig,* formed the core of the khan's military and administrative organization; they were recruited from the sons of high-ranking commanders as well as from among talented commoner nomads.

In May 1204 (dated with unusual precision in the *Secret History,* evidence that the compiler had some official records, Chinese or Persian, to consult for this episode), the Mongol army rode forth along the Kerulen River westward toward the Naiman base in the Altai Mountains. A greatly embellished *Secret History* narrative preserves an epic account of Mongol military ingenuity (overcoming fatigue and puny numbers through stratagem), Tayang khan's craven retreat, Jamukha's predictable scams, and the tragic end of the doomed Naiman soldiers. Temüjin's men bottled up the main Naiman force on a spiny precipice; they panicked: "Tumbling down from the height of Naqu Cliff, they piled on top of each other; they fell breaking their bones and died crushing each other till they were like heaps of rotten logs." Tayang khan perished; his son and heir Küchlüg escaped to his uncle, Buyirukh khan. Jamukha and most of the Merkits again fled the field of battle rather than submit.

Haughty queen Gürbesü entered the conqueror's household as a secondary consort, after she passed his inspection: "You used to say that the Mongols have a bad smell, didn't you? Why, then, did you come now?" More prominent was Khulan-khatun, the daughter offered to Temüjin by a defeated Merkit leader. She became a principal wife, heading the first rank attached to the second *ordo* or palace encampment (in later Mongolian chronicles, she turns into a Korean princess). She and her son born to Chinggis Khan appear in many documents of the thirteenth century. Her son died in Russia during Mongol campaigns there.

The Mongols moved to wipe up Jamukha's tribal allies, and to chase down and annihilate the Merkits under Temüjin's old enemy, Toghto'a-beki. Toghto'a eluded them once more, fleeing west across the Altai Mountains to link up with Küchlüg and Buyirukh khan. It took several more years to track down and eliminate the Naiman and Merkit holdouts. Late in 1208, with the help of Oirat guides, Mongol troops fought them along the upper course of the Irtysh River. Toghto'a-beki at last fell; his sons scattered in all directions seeking refuge where they could. Naiman prince Küchlüg got away with some companions and headed south into central Asia, like his Kereyit counterpart, though he exceeded the latter in luck and cunning, and ended up occupying (with Merkit support!) the Qara

Khitai throne for a while. Finally, in ca. 1218 (the date is disputed) his adventures ended at the sword of the Mongol warrior Jebe. Perhaps because of their resistance to incorporation into the Mongol federation, later in the thirteenth century the Naimans, like the Tanguts, ended up being classified in Chinese sources not as "Mongols" but as *semu*, or western and central Asian foreign experts employed by the Mongols to rule China. This Yuan dynasty legal designation placed them one step below the Mongol ruling class, which otherwise included former Merkits, Tatars, Kereyits, and other inhabitants of the Mongolian plateau united under Chinggis Khan.

How Jamukha met his end varies in the telling. The *Secret History* presents a parable of justice: Handed over to Temüjin by his own companions, who were immediately slain for that duplicity, Jamukha refused Temüjin's pleas to join him again and begged to be put to death for his crimes against his sworn brother. His bones, he promised Temüjin, "shall protect you and be a blessing to the offspring of your offspring." Acquiescing, Temüjin ordered that Jamukha die without shedding blood and be buried in style. Rashid al-Din, perhaps more reliably, records a bloodier demise: Restrained from executing Jamukha himself by their *anda* vows, Temüjin turned him over to his youngest brother, who had the man hacked to death. Given Jamukha's long history of treachery, the *Secret History* account should be understood as a literary elaboration on the justice of Temüjin's sentence of death for the friend who acknowledged his unforgivable violation of a sacred trust. Jamukha was out of the picture by the 1206 coronation of Temüjin as Chinggis Khan.

Heaven's Destiny

Although in hindsight it seems inevitable that Temüjin would subdue all of the tribes on the Mongolian plateau, it took another decade or more to incorporate the forest tribes north of the plateau, around Lake Baikal, and some degree of tribal resistance or backsliding forever shadowed the Mongol enterprise. Nevertheless, by 1205 the heartland of the great nomadic empires of bygone ages had been unified by a Mongol khan, seemingly the least likely of its occupants to do so. Rashid al-Din cites a minor Mongol clansman who offered this assessment of the various candidates for leadership:

> Sacha-beki of the... Jurkin seeks supremacy, but he is not up to it. Jamukha-sechen* will not succeed either, for he is always setting people against one another and seeks to advance his cause through machination and deceit. Jochi-bara [Temüjin's brother Khasar] has the same ambition, and relies on his strength and skill with the bow, but he too will not succeed. Nor will anything come of the Merkit Alakh-udur's pursuit of preeminence, despite his display of power and grandeur. It is Temüjin who possesses the mien, the conduct, and the acumen necessary to dominate and to rule, and he will without doubt achieve the position of sovereign.

*Sechen "the wise," a common sobriquet attached to Mongol names.

Jamukha's challenge to Temüjin has been magnified to monopolize the storyline in the *Secret History* and some other sources, masking dissension within the hero's household. Seeing Khasar in the ranks of contenders helps to explain some of the oblique references to bad feeling between the brothers. The sibling rivalry did not go away, as subsequent events testify. Later Mongol chronicles elaborate it extensively, although how reliably we cannot know. Brothers normally went their separate ways in the course of daily life on the steppe, so being forced into subservience to one's indomitable elder brother understandably placed strains on their relationship.

We will likewise never know whether Temüjin himself held a firm conviction of his own Heaven-endorsed candidacy at that time, or those beliefs were only later attributed to him owing to his unusual luck. No doubt truth lies in both.

By the spring of 1205 (Ox year), Temüjin controlled the Orkhon River valley and the Mongolian plateau. His path southward into Tangut territory, north China, and central Asia lay open (see Maps 7.1 and 8.1). In search of booty to supply his growing establishment and replenish the herds after winter, and perhaps to scout out the land through which Ong-khan's son, Senggüm, had recently fled, Temüjin authorized a spring raiding expedition southward into Hexi (west of the [Yellow] River), the Tangut Xia lands. Under the command of Yelu Ahai, a Khitan, the raiding party attacked several western Tangut border towns and returned with camels, cattle, and captives. Certainly no later than 1205, then, and likely before, both Khitans and Tanguts were entering into Mongol service.

Yelu Ahai first met Temüjin some years earlier during his residence at Ong-khan's court in the late 1190s as an envoy from the Jurchen capital in north China. His Chinese biography reports that impressed with the Mongol chieftain and desiring to serve him, Ahai returned a year later with his younger brother as a pledge of loyalty to Temüjin. Both brothers were at Baljuna. Yelu Ahai knew several languages (Chinese, Khitan, and Jurchen, at least) and possibly was able to advise Temüjin on the state of Tangut–Kereyit relations (Jakha Gambu had also married a daughter to the Tangut emperor), conditions in north China or at least along the frontier, and the best way to take advantage of the vulnerabilities and opportunities in these areas.

By the early thirteenth century, nearly fifty years of peaceful relations among the three settled powers south of the Gobi—Xia, Jin, and Song—had begun to unravel. North of the Gobi, the recent steppe wars had sent tremors through the Eurasian frontier. Some Khitans, former masters of the north Asian steppe, had reestablished their Liao state out in central Asia in the mid-twelfth century under the name of Qara Khitai; others stayed to serve their conquerors, the Jurchen Jin. Increasingly dissatisfied with Jin frontier policies, these Khitans now began to take up service with the Mongols, whose language and culture they shared and to whom they brought the critical expertise gained in north China. They were the most influential of the Mongols' early advisors. Yelu Ahai may have attended the great *khuriltai* (assembly) of 1206 to celebrate his new master's rise to power.

Temüjin's coronation in 1206 was more than a celebration of his achievements; it marked a structural turning point, which required an ideological adjustment as well. In Chapter 6, we will examine the structures that emerged with the formalization of Chinggis Khan's assumption of supreme rule in Mongolia, and assess the nature of change and continuity to which they bear witness.

6

Organizing the Empire, 1205–1210

When one has been raised to the rank of beki, he shall wear a white dress and ride a white gelding, he shall sit on a high seat and be waited upon.

—THE SECRET HISTORY OF THE MONGOLS

In the spring of 1206, Year of the Tiger, Temüjin summoned his kinfolk, close companions, commanders, and leaders of the subordinate tribes and clans to a *khuriltai* at the source of the Onon River, near the sacred mountain Burkhan Khaldun, home of the Mongols' earliest ancestors. There the assembled steppe aristocrats, new and old, raised the "white standard with nine tails" and elected Temüjin their khan, with the new name of *Chinggis*, "The Fierce." The white standard with nine streamers made from horse or yak tails had become Chinggis's exclusive symbol of power and sovereignty, both the color white and the number nine being auspicious to the Altaic peoples. (The color black was associated with commoner status.) As a symbol of Heaven's favor, the source of his good fortune, it validated his right to their loyalty as overlord of all the "peoples of the felt tents."

The name (not title) *Chinggis* has spawned various explanations and translations. Igor de Rachewiltz, whose translation of the *Secret History* is followed here, argues for "fierce, hard, tough." Rashid al-Din understood it as equivalent to the Persian title *shah-an-shah* ("shah of shahs"), although it was only after his death that Chinggis retrospectively gained the title *khaghan* ("khan of khans" or Great Khan, also spelled *qa'an*). Most accounts relate that the name *Chinggis* was bestowed on Temüjin by a member of his retinue, Teb Tenggeri (Lord Divine), supposedly a shaman. We will return to his story later. Archaeological digs of the 1950s have uncovered the site of Chinggis Khan's base camp in Khentii Province of northeastern Mongolia, called Awarga, possibly from the medieval term for "base camp," *aurug.*

The ancient Turkic titles *khan* and *khaghan*, commonly understood as "king" or "emperor," had been in use since the early centuries CE among the inner Asian steppe peoples. Rulers of the sixth- to eighth-century Turk Empires styled themselves khaghans, but when the Khitans, one of their subject peoples, rose to power in the tenth century they dropped that title to assume the supreme Chinese designation of *huangdi*, "emperor." Their successors in central Asia, the Qara Khitai, continued to call their rulers emperors but also adopted the inner Asian title *gürkhan* (universal khan), and titles of Arabo-Persian origin appear as well in the Muslim sources for the Qara Khitai. Chinggis Khan's third son and successor, Ögedei, assumed the Mongolian equivalent of *khaghan*, calling himself *kha'an* (*qa'an*), and subsequently that title was bestowed retroactively on his father. From then on all rulers at the Mongol Empire's center became Great Khans, while their relatives presiding over khanates in Persia, Russia, and central Asia ruled as local khans, theoretically subordinate to the Great Khan.

The reforms described later took place over several years, some beginning before 1206, some after. In many cases they followed steppe precedents, enriched by the experiences of the Uighurs, Naimans, Kereyits, and Khitans, among others. What distinguished the Mongols from previous steppe rulers was the scope of their control and the impact of their reorganizing enterprise on the steppe world itself, quite apart from the later incorporation of sedentary lands and the extension of their governing techniques over distant though not occupied territories. As Thomas Allsen has succinctly summarized, "[t]his reordering of steppe society enabled the Mongols, for the first time in history, to impose a single, centralized authority across the whole of the steppe zone and thereby monopolize and mobilize its chief military resource—equestrian archers." That authority remained centralized just long enough to power the conquest establishment for decades.

Military Organization and Social Structure: Army, Guards, and Tribes

According to the *Secret History*, one of the first acts of the new khan was to reward loyal followers with appointment, or reappointment, as commander (*noyan*) of a thousand (chiliarch). The newly appointed (or confirmed) commanders, many of whom hailed from humble stations in the old steppe society, now filled the ranks of a powerful elite. Chinggis handed out ninety-five such appointments, all named in the *Secret History*, attesting to the growth of Mongol manpower following unification of the tribes. Senior among them, Mukhali and Bo'orchu also received command over ten thousand troops, a myriarchy or *tümen* (ten chiliarchies), becoming generals of the Right (western) and Left (eastern) wings of the Mongol army, respectively (from a southern orientation, west and east become right and left).

Bo'orchu's own regiment of a thousand was made up of men of his own tribe, a special honor, and constituted the first unit in the Right Wing. Likewise, as the first unit in the Left Wing, Mukhali controlled a chiliarchy of his own Jalayir tribesmen, originally hereditary serfs of the Jurkins (Chinggis's relatives). In Mukhali's case, because Left Wing troops generally came from tribes in eastern and central Mongolia, the campaign against north China fell under his jurisdiction and command. Chinggis also created a myriarchy of the center under a trusted Tayichi'ut. These were the units that accompanied him on campaign, along with his *keshig* or imperial guard.

By around 1206, then, the Mongols could muster ninety-five regiments of a thousand men each, theoretically. We should not read the names "*thousand*" or "*ten thousand*" as a literal measure of the command's strength; these regiments seldom furnished much more than half of a full complement of troops. More prestigious and trusted commanders undoubtedly had more men under their authority.

To supplement the ninety-five "thousands" and meet the enlarged administrative needs of the Mongols, Chinggis expanded the guard, the most important component of Mongol government, which combined civil/administrative and military functions. His original guard, or *keshig*, grew from about one thousand to ten thousand men or ten chiliarchies, divided as before into day and night guards. As before, guard members were recruited from the sons and brothers of the commanders of a thousand (*noyan*) as well as from talented nomad commoners under those generals. In addition, foreign youths entered the guards as pledges of loyalty from rulers who submitted to the Mongol khan, a time-honored arrangement that fulfilled one of the requirements of surrender. There they received the training and experience that usually turned them into steadfast servants of the khan. Guard members thus formed a cadre of "hostage sons" whose special position close to the khan guaranteed the loyalty of their families, their own careers, and the khan's access to a pool of trusted talent. In this way, the formative years of the empire's core institutions allowed for a degree of social mobility in the recruitment of guardsmen and other skilled commoners, but the importance of rank, status, and seniority in apportioning resources did not encourage movement from one level to the next in the stratified hierarchy of the ruling elite.

Although the Mongols kept their troop strength secret, estimates for 1206 based on the figures mentioned earlier range from a high of ninety-five thousand to a more likely fifty thousand to seventy-five thousand soldiers. By the end of Chinggis's reign, troop strength had grown to about 129,000, largely as a result of the absorption of sedentary and other nomadic elements. The purely Mongol proportion of the mounted cavalry remained small, and some of the Mongols' most legendary military feats were accomplished under famed commanders such as Jebe and Sübetei with thirty thousand or fewer men.

The imperial guards comprised an elite unit, responsible for both household and military tasks. They took care of the khan's family, his daily needs, his possessions, and his safety, serving in strictly regulated rotation of duty shifts. When a khan died, his *keshig* tended his home *ordo*, or palace tents, and the new khan recruited his own guard. Because everything the Mongols conquered—peoples, lands, and wealth—constituted the khan's "property" (more properly, the property of the royal lineage), the scope of *keshig* authority was wide indeed: It administered the empire. Wherever the khan traveled, there went the *keshig*. The logistical challenge can be imagined and over time generated a host of new institutions.

The rise of the Mongol Empire entailed a dramatic transformation of relationships among its constituent members, as well as the militarization of Mongol society. Most of the conquered tribespeople were split up and distributed among the new military regiments, and thereby acquired a new ethnopolitical identity. In a few cases, Chinggis awarded trustworthy servitors, such as Bo'orchu and Mukhali (formerly a "threshold slave" in Temüjin's camp), with permission to form a regiment from their own clan or tribesfolk, thus allowing those groups to remain intact. Sübetei and Jebe, two of Chinggis's "four hounds," likewise peopled their chiliarchies with subordinate tribesmen. The domestic life of rank-and-file warriors too came under their commander's purview; indeed his fighting effectiveness and mobility stemmed from a commander's authority over the nomads, as well as their families and herds, who provided the backbone of the Mongol army. The commander held that authority in exchange for maintaining absolute military discipline and loyalty to the khan. A commander's post could pass on to his offspring, but it could also revert to the khan and be reassigned to another man if he failed in his duties. A new society was emerging.

At some point, probably in ca. 1210, this new supratribal polity began to use the name *Yeke Mongol Ulus*, or "Great Mongol Nation," following the custom of other states ruling in east Asia. We can now refer to all of the disparate peoples united under the khan's rule as "Mongols," although their original affiliations are remembered and recorded in the sources. Chinggis's reforms aimed to institutionalize their detachment from previous tribal affinities and redirect their loyalties and service obligations exclusively toward himself, by way of his loyal commanders. Thus he instigated a cycle or process of detribalization and centralization unprecedented in steppe history, creating a new social hierarchy with his family and close associates as the ruling class. In other words, one feature that distinguished the Mongol Empire from past steppe empires was the extent of societal mobilization, near total, under the khan.

It is sometimes tempting to overstate the degree to which Chinggis succeeded in splitting up established tribes; indeed we have seen earlier that some of his *noyan* kept their tribal kin together under their commands. However, no one disputes his success in realigning loyalties. If a degree of social engineering occurred in these years, it did not eliminate tribes as a basic sociopolitical unit, though it did redefine their membership or create new tribal units altogether. A gradual process of "retribalization" took place when the empire dissolved in the fourteenth century as the original decimal superstructure that supplied the great khan's armies dispersed into regional entities around Eurasia. Retribalization did not simply restore groups that had existed in the twelfth century; rather it created new tribes or peoples, some using the old names but with significantly altered membership. Highly ranked clans, however, tended to retain positions of privilege in these new groupings and in the regional khanates.

Having placed his trusted warriors in positions of authority second only to his, Chinggis bestowed special privileges on particular companions who had performed heroic deeds in bringing him to power: for Father Mönglik, permission to sit in a place of honor inside his tent, on the immediate right of the khan; for others, bestowal of favored women. To Mukhali, Bo'orchu, and other worthies, the khan granted the right to sit "above all others" on ceremonial occasions (i.e., on a bench below the khan's elevated platform but above the assembly seated on the ground), and the "nine-fold pardon," an extraordinary legal dispensation that exempted the holder from punishment for up to nine infractions of the law. The khan's laws were widely believed by later folks to have been enshrined in his *Yasakh*, or law code, though no document by that name has survived.

Sometimes conflated with "the sayings of Chinggis," as far as we know the *Yasakh* consisted of the pronouncements by the first and perhaps next two Mongol khans, principally on matters of military discipline, the hunt, and the postal system (*jam*, probably established under Ögedei, Chinggis's successor). What matters is that Chinggis and his retinue brought order to an unruly society. Punishments decreed for disobedience were fairly draconian: execution for robbery and adultery, for example. Groups stood responsible for individual crimes; if a man bolted in battle, his entire unit of ten men suffered punishment. Feuding, plundering, kidnapping of women, and brawling, which were common from their childhood, more or less ceased for the time being. John of Plano Carpini, a papal envoy who traveled to the Mongols' imperial encampment in 1245–1247, echoes a common perception of European sojourners among the Mongols:

> Fights, brawls, wounding, murder are never met with among them. Nor are robbers and thieves who steal on a large scale found there. . . . if any animals are lost, whoever comes across them either leaves them alone or takes them to men appointed for this purpose. . . . They show considerable respect to each other and are very friendly together. . .

From then on violence would be directed outward in a controlled fashion. Thus Chinggis whipped the ragtag, rowdy and pugnacious nomads lovingly depicted in the *Secret History* into a well-tempered war machine. This accomplishment, and the methods and principles devised to perpetuate it, including generous treatment of loyal followers, may be thought of as the "Great Yasakh," which was held in reverence by the steppe rulers down through the centuries, or invoked opportunistically to serve their own ends.

All these new edicts, dispensations, and regulations needed to be recorded, filed, and recalled reliably, giving birth to Mongol-style bureaucracy (unloved by the Chinese, who invented bureaucracy) and a writing system for Mongolian. Chinggis Khan had already pondered the usefulness of writing, no later than the Naiman campaign of 1204. One of the captives of that battle, Tata-tonga, was a literate Uighur serving as the Naiman seal-keeper. When he explained to his new overlord what the seal was used for (we read in his Chinese biography, not surprisingly), Chinggis appointed the man to start using a seal on all *his* subsequent decrees, and moreover to teach the Uighur writing used in the Naiman and Kereyit administrations to all the Mongol princes. The vertical, alphabetical

Uighur script (derived from Syriac via Sogdian, an ancient central Asian script) thus became the first written medium of the Mongols' language.

Also literate in Uighur was Chinggis's adopted son, Shigi-khutukhu, who admittedly may have learned to write from Tata-tonga along with khan's other sons. In 1206 or perhaps some years later, Chinggis appointed Shigi-khutukhu, another bearer of the "nine-fold pardon," to serve as chief judge (*jarghuchi*) and record-keeper:

> Of the entire people—curbing theft, discouraging falsehood—execute those who deserve death, punish those who deserve punishment. Furthermore, writing in a blue-script register all decisions about distribution and about the judicial matters of the entire population, make it into a book. Until the offspring of my offspring, let no one alter any of the blue writing. . . .

From this originated the Mongols' "Blue Book" (*köke debter*), the first internal official record of Mongol affairs and legal precedents as well as a population register. In addition to keeping the "Blue Book," Shigi-khutukhu's duties included supervising the allocation of subject peoples, adjudicating crimes, and sentencing the condemned, with the assistance of *keshig* personnel.

The "Golden Lineage": Property, Inheritance, and Succession in the Royal Clan

The Borjigin clan to which Chinggis Khan belonged became known as the "Golden Lineage" (*altan urukh*); only its members, or more narrowly the descendants of Chinggis's sons, could be elected as khans. The number of lineage members multiplied rapidly over the decades, if we count all its dependent women, children, slaves, and servitors. However indebted Chinggis was to his family's support, succeeding as a khan and satisfying the customary expectations of close kin presented a series of contradictions, which many of the anecdotes in the *Secret History* aim to resolve. Tensions at the family level mirrored the contradictions between maintaining a supratribal polity (a nomadic empire) and satisfying the daily needs of pastoral nomads. In short, the Borjigins expected to fully share in the spoils of conquest, while the khan needed to assert his absolute authority over everyone in order to mobilize the resources necessary to keep himself in power. In theory the empire belonged to the family, and major decisions regarding its future necessitated consultation with all shareholders at a *khuriltai*. In practice, a successful khan made decisions after consulting his most trusted non-kin *noyan* as well as senior relatives, and convoked a *khuriltai* to announce and affirm those decisions. In addition to expanding his patrimony, Chinggis had to plan for its future, and he gave careful thought to how best to preserve it when his time expired. Transmission of property and transmission of leadership, after all, invoked two different and conflicting sets of principles.

In or shortly after 1206, Chinggis Khan apportioned subject peoples to his mother, surviving brothers, adoptive brothers (the other boys put in his mother's care), senior sons by his primary wife Börte (Jochi, Chaghadai, Ögedei, and Tolui), other sons (adopted or of secondary wives), and other female relatives (wives, daughters, and others). These grants, normally with pasturelands to accommodate the requirements of a pastoral livelihood, constituted the core of an individual's *ulus* ("people") or appanage, and supplied sustenance, labor, and military or defensive needs. Note the emphasis on people, rather than land, as the principle resource. Where land was inseparable from people (e.g., farmers or pastureland), the two might overlap, but this was not always the case. Over time further conquests enlarged some of the grants, and the largest, contiguous uluses evolved into separate khanates (states ruled by khans). But that was not part of Chinggis Khan's original vision.

Royal family members, wherever their main *ordo* (palace encampment) might lie, supplemented their incomes through heritable shares in the booty or tax revenues generated from conquered territories, and they designated representatives to accompany conquest armies in order to stake their claims. We see this practice in place by no later than 1218–1219. Thereafter, whenever, possible Borjigin agents traveled hither and yon across the Eurasian continent, collecting the monies or goods owing to their masters, regardless of how friendly or hostile the rulers of the territories happened to be at the moment. Il-khanid royals routinely collected tax receipts from "fiefs" in north China, for example. Nor did Golden kin scruple to grab bits of other Golden Family properties, should the opportunity arise. Imagine a multinational corporation, whose shareholders travel around its constituent enterprises to gather dividends, even when the board of governors has fallen to quarrelling or is engaged in sabotage or pitched battle. Imagine shareholders and executives filching from one another's stocks. The Mongols would have been at home on Wall Street, but in their case, it was an extension of the custom of economic democracy among elites, not a violation of public trust.

At this time, between 1206 and 1210, Chinggis's youngest brother, Temüge-otchigin, and their mother together received some eight or ten thousand people, which Hö'elün found a paltry return for her pains. By custom, the youngest son (otchigin) inherited the home (hearth) and herds of his parents and cared for them in their old age. Furthermore, Chinggis evidently did not think enough of his younger brother to assign him to posts outside Mongolia. The khan's other brothers netted even smaller portions (Khasar, four thousand; Belgütei, one thousand five hundred). Khasar and his descendants also made their base in the northeast, east of the Mongols' homeland. Normally the eldest son took his share of the property (animals, usually) first and went farthest from the home camp to make his living. As the eldest son, Chinggis was still expanding his share. In any case, the khan deliberately did not furnish his brothers with greater resources than his sons, to whom he planned to leave his life's work.

To elder son Jochi, Chinggis allotted nine thousand people; to Chaghadai eight thousand, and to the third and fourth sons, Ögedei and Tolui, five thousand each. Ögedei ended up becoming the next khan, so later inherited the empire. The territorial bases of the khan's eldest and youngest sons, Jochi and Tolui, shifted over time. Although Jochi's sons ended up ruling the Qipchaq steppe (the Golden Horde) from a base south of Kiev, which was indeed the farthest from the "homeland," his early territories lay considerably east and north of southern Russia. Tolui, Chinggis's "otchigin," inherited the homeland territories in eastern Mongolia (the "Center") but seldom dwelled there, and his sons ended up all over the map: Hülegü in Persia, Möngke and Khubilai in China and the "Center," Arik Böke in the Altai Mountains of western Mongolia (see Map 6.1.) Descendants of the second son, Chaghadai, got squeezed on all sides, especially from Ögedei's grandson, who used central Asia as a base from which to challenge the rule of Khubilai in China. By the mid-thirteenth century, the picture had become exceedingly complex. (See the Genealogical and Reign Chart for a schematic representation of the divisions among the Golden Lineage.)

The closest equivalent to economic democracy (not equality) among elites in the political realm of an autocratic khan was the tradition that the brothers, uncles, and nephews of a chief were all legitimate candidates for succession to the chief's position. Within a tribe, the presiding elders might agree amicably about who should become the new chief. At the higher levels of federation or empire, with more at stake, the matter often had to be decided through a

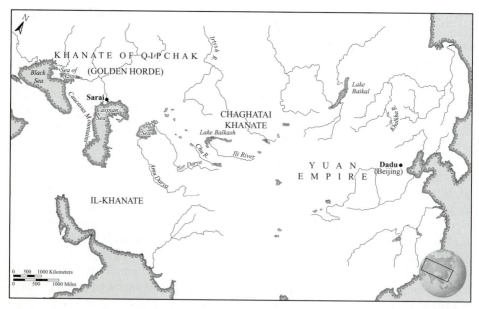

Map 6.1 Mongol Empire, ca. 1279

lengthy process of elimination in battle and factional maneuvering, during which the weaker candidates fell by the wayside, leaving the strongest and cleverest as the new khan, acclaimed by all at a *khuriltai* (assembly). Temüjin fought long and hard to become both tribal and supratribal khan. Khasar's troubled relationship with his older brother and reputation as a superb bowman suggest that the mighty archer had also harbored dreams of leading his tribe to glory. Another pretender sought to exploit the tensions between Khasar and the khan.

All sources tell us that the khan received the name *Chinggis* from Teb Tenggeri, the fourth son of Father Mönglik. Mönglik, the son of a companion of Yisügei who fetched nine-year old Temüjin back from his bride's camp and who might have become Hö'elün's second husband, the khan's trusty old household retainer, first named commander of a thousand, holder of the "nine-fold pardon" and honored member of the inner circle—practically a member of the family—had seven sons (presumably not with Hö'elün). In the drama narrated by the *Secret History*, Teb Tenggeri's overweening pride in his supernatural and prophetic powers emboldened him to challenge his khan. He corralled his brawny siblings to beat up and humiliate Chinggis's brothers, alienated some of their subject peoples, and insinuated to the khan that Khasar was plotting against him. Disarmed by Teb Tenggeri's apparent open channel to the compass of his destiny (Heaven or Tengri), and willing to suspect Khasar, Chinggis did not act. The abuse continued. Only the intervention of Börte forced Chinggis to acknowledge the challenge and to rein in Teb Tenggeri. The khan permitted his injured youngest brother to seize and kill the shaman by severing his spine (the honorable death).

Later writers have called Teb Tenggeri a shaman and interpret the incident as a conflict between priestly and political authorities. Superstitious, the steppe nomads stood in awe of the powers of their shamans to heal, predict, identify auspicious days to begin a battle or hunt, restore women's fertility, grant heavenly names, and communicate generally with the spirit world. Chinggis's resolution, in this view, was to destroy the priest and arrogate his powers to himself, while appointing a new but nominal head shaman. On the other hand, nothing could be more natural than that there were influential men in Chinggis's retinue—no, in his very family—such as Khasar and Teb Tenggeri, not content to play second fiddle to an increasingly autocratic khan.

The incident prompted Chinggis to reduce Khasar's allotment of subject peoples (from four thousand to one thousand four hundred), further disappointing his elderly mother so that she died soon after. Father Mönglik did not suffer any worse consequences than a lecture about parenting:

> By not restraining your sons' nature, you and your sons began thinking that you were equal to me, and you have paid for this with Teb Tenggeri's life. Had I known that you had such a nature, you would have been dealt with like Jamukha, Altan, Kuchar and the others. So he railed at Father Monglik. . . . And, his anger abated, he showed favour to him again.

But the influence of Father Monglik and his sons thereafter declined. No further challenges to Chinggis appeared from within. In the coming years his stature gained such weight and aura that he alone of all the Mongol khans named his successor before he died.

Belief, Custom, and Justification: Early Mongol Ideology

The various measures elaborated earlier laid the foundation of the empire that evolved over the next several decades. As the horsemen moved out of the Mongolian plateau down into the heart of Eurasia, these institutions and practices evolved as need arose. If iron nomad discipline and a decimal-based military organization enabled astonishing military victories, what prompted and then justified them?

It is impossible for us to know what Temüjin thought he was doing and why, since we have only other peoples' word for it. The *Secret History*, with its legends of divine genesis, is clearly the product of later propagandists aiming to buttress the claims of Chinggisid rulers. From their words, however, we can deduce a fair amount. We saw earlier that Chinggis Khan deployed various symbols to manifest his (and his lineage's) just claim to rule over all the steppe peoples, and that Heaven and luck figured centrally in explanations of his early successes. What was the nature of this Mongol Heaven? When and where did the idea of conquering other lands beyond the steppes come from? What was the link between intertribal feuding and world conquest?

A reverence for Tengri or "eternal blue Heaven" (*köke möngke tenggeri*) was widely shared among the steppe nomads since ancient times. In the *Secret History*, it figures as a kind of deity, a sky god, presiding over the mundane and supramundane worlds, the latter populated with largely hostile spirits or "demons" (in Christian European eyes) of every kind, which the shamans propitiated or neutralized. Given the ecological difficulties and brutality of steppe life, survival ipso facto exhibited the presence of Heaven's favor. The longer one survived conditions of danger (abandonment, cold, hunger, theft, abduction, chase, betrayal, piercing by arrows, and battle defeat) the weightier grew the hand of Heaven's favor (*kut*). In the political (i.e., military) realm, Tengri favored winners. This was not only a personal psychological prop but persuaded others to align themselves with you, on the side of Heaven, and fostered the development of a steppe political tradition of divinely decreed sovereignty.

The concept of a Heavenly appointed monarch suggests influence from the Chinese theory of the "mandate of Heaven" (*tian ming*), which would-be kings had to prove they held in order to turn a rebellion into a legitimate new dynasty. Probably both share a common derivation, but regardless, medieval Turk notions of *tenggeri* (the Turk spelling) would be the immediate source of Mongol ideas about Heaven, not China. Tengri, like the Chinese idea of a "mandate of Heaven," could be manipulated by politically astute aspirants to power. Teb Tenggeri perhaps calculated that he could win over Chinggis Khan's supporters on the strength of his ability to communicate directly with Heaven. Moreover, it has been argued that the Mongol notion of Tengri became over the thirteenth century increasingly monotheistic under the widening influence of Christianity and Islam, which may have imbued its earthly sovereign with qualities of omnipotence and universality not fully realized in earlier steppe deployments of Heavenly legitimation. In the 1240s, John of Plano Carpini noted that the Mongols whom he encountered were worshipping Chinggis Khan:

> They have also made an idol to the first Emperor, which they have placed in a cart in a place of honour before a dwelling, as we saw before the present Emperor's court, and they offer gifts to it. . . . They bow to it towards the south as to God, and they make other nobles who are visiting them do the same.

Such understanding of their sky deity was buttressed by Chinggis Khan's occupation of the Orkhon River valley in central Mongolia, the traditional center of earlier steppe empires. Carved on massive stones erected in the Orkhon valley by the last of the Eastern Turk kaghans and their Uighur successors, the eighth-century runic Turk inscriptions elaborate the ideology of the imperial Turks who reigned over a vast central Asian empire from the sixth century to the eighth century. The Mongols regarded themselves as heirs to the legacy of the imperial Turks, and to the residual good fortune adhering in the valley, surrounded by the Turks' sacred mountains, for that was the site Chinggis Khan choose for the future imperial capital of Kharakhorum. The Mongols' own sacred mountain to the east, Burkhan Khaldun, became instead the Golden Lineage's burial ground.

Chinggis Khan's vision of his destiny and his determination to protect the integrity of his accomplishment could, under the right circumstances, propel the united Mongols outward. The circumstances were indeed right—ecological, economic, political, social, and cultural. Yet one must resist the temptation to assume, from later outcomes, that this is what the Mongols were planning for in 1206.

Scholars have speculated on the impact of climatic change (a drop in the mean annual temperature, drought), possible overpopulation given the fragility of the pastoral economy, and a decline in trade with sedentary societies to supplement food supplies as contributing factors in the outward expansion of the early thirteenth-century Mongols. Survival was tenuous, as the khan's childhood illustrates. Amidst the deprivations of life on the twelfth-century Mongolian steppes, a cultural logic of survival animated Temüjin and his society. That logic was about feuds, vengeance, and the community of brotherhood that the obligation of vengeance created, strengthened, or destroyed. Justice demanded restitution for slights or insults resulting in the loss of respect, not to mention horses, family members, or precious supplies. Temüjin's community of brotherhood waxed and waned, but eventually grew in numbers as well as in right, or virtue, as he moved to restore justice by avenging one by one the wrongs perpetrated on his ancestors, family (including sworn father, Ong-khan), and self. In addition to the requirement to avenge a wrong, absolute loyalty came to be an inflexible virtue. In the course of punishing disloyal friends and their allies, Temüjin had already come up against the sedentary world, which harbored rebels against Mongol justice. Later, when he warred against the Jurchen Jin, he justified it as vengeance for Jin mistreatment of earlier Mongol khans. From the cultural logic of the feud to imperial conquest lay a seemingly short and seamless step.

Chinggis Khan, generous as well as practical, knew that the virtues of loyalty and demands of vengeance were expensive to cultivate; followers must be rewarded, warriors must be fed. The ability to distribute largesse defined one of the essential attributes of a khan. To stay in power meant to continue seeking booty, and the local supply of cattle, foodstuffs, essential materiel, and dainties was limited. Here was the "cry" of "insatiable hunger" of a new-born steppe empire. The khan had to look elsewhere to secure the economic underpinnings of his power.

Yet the world out there was unknown, alien, and hostile, judging by relations with Jin. How best to position oneself in relation to it? The Mongols loved the steppes; they cherished the ability to hop on a horse and ride off into the distance. They had no particular desire to settle down to indolence in the palaces of Samarqand or Kaifeng, and they looked down on sedentary folk as by and large unfortunate slaves. As Chinggis Khan came to interpret his divinely ordained mission in the world over the remaining decades of his life, everyone out there owed him fealty and, in return for the grace of his sovereignty, should surrender to him their finest products, animals, young men and women, and obedience. So into the world he sent scouts, raiding parties, trade delegations, and armies. The particular train of events that these initiatives unleashed nicely illustrates the contingency of history, as well as the steppe ruler's deployment of trade and raid (or punishment, in the case of the Jin) as revenue-collecting strategies.

7

Opening a Southern Front: The First China Campaigns, 1207–1218

We shall weave woolen material and make satin, and we shall give them to you. Training falcons to fly loose at game, we shall gather them and all the best ones we shall send to you.

—THE SECRET HISTORY OF THE MONGOLS

Unification of the northern steppes under a forceful and ambitious khan did not happen even once in every century. When it did, the shrewder local rulers hastened to assess their own position vis-à-vis the rising power. In particular, the destruction of the Naiman and Merkit federations and the flight of their princes into central Asia, as described in Chapter 4, set off alarms throughout the Qara Khitai realm. Although Küchlüg, the Naiman heir, managed to usurp the Qara Khitai throne within three years of his expulsion from Mongolia, eliminating Qara Khitai power in central Asia was not on Chinggis Khan's agenda. Rather, to consolidate the Mongols' accomplishment and confront the Jin state in north China, he took up several tasks during this decade: suppressing the slippery Merkit and Naiman princes (who might be organizing resistance to the Mongol rear), securing the submission of tribes beyond the Mongolian plateau, neutralizing or winning over the Tangut Xia state, and finally forcing the Jin to pay tribute to him, instead of the other way around. There is no evidence that the Mongols yet dreamed to conquer north China. But by the end of the decade, the first task would bring them into confrontation with a host of hostile successors to the Qara Khitai ruler.

After 1206 Mongol envoys traveled to tribes still outside their confederation, and a series of submissions followed: The Kirghiz (west of Lake Baikal) returned an embassy bearing white falcons in 1207 and the Oirats (southwest of Lake Baikal) tendered allegiance in 1208, after helping Mongol forces to track fugitive Merkit and Naiman nobles. (These and other "Forest Peoples" of south Siberia later rebelled, were subdued in 1218–1219 by Jochi, and became his subjects [see Map 2.1].)

More consequential to Chinggis Khan's future, the Uighur ruler Barchukh Art Tegin readily acknowledged his suzerainty. As vassals of the Qara Khitai since ca. 1130, the urbane Uighurs had been left unbothered until the early thirteenth century, when the hand of the gürkhan's rule grew heavy in decline. Having just murdered an oppressive monk-official deputed to collect taxes from the Uighurs, Barchukh received the Mongol khan's envoy gladly in 1209, hoping for his help in discarding Qara Khitai dominion. When later that year the homeless Merkit princes sought refuge in Uighur territory, Barchukh's forces expelled them in a show of good faith to Chinggis Khan. In return for his pledge to serve Chinggis as a "son," the khan gave Barchukh a daughter in marriage when the Uighur king presented himself to his new overlord in 1211.

Likewise, by the spring of 1211 a Mongol expedition into central Asia tracking the Naiman and Merkit refugees had won over the Arslan (Lion) Khan, chief of the Muslim Qarluq Turks in the lower Ili valley south of Lake Balkash (see Map 8.1). Refusing to acknowledge the Naiman pretender to the Qara Khitai throne, Arslan tendered submission to Chinggis Khan. Voluntary submission put the rulers of the Önggüts, Uighurs, and Qarluqs in the privileged ranks of royal sons-in-law. These important Turkic peoples from the southern Gobi to the heart of central Asia furnished manpower for the Mongol armies. In addition, the literate and sophisticated Uighurs (the most sedentarized of the Turks) supplied administrators for the expanding empire.

Furthermore, whenever a ruler or his agents appeared before the khan to offer submission, whether voluntarily or coerced, the ceremony included a presentation of gifts by the new vassal: the best, costliest, most precious objects he (or his people) possessed. Their gifts supplemented the booty filling Chinggis Khan's treasuries, and a certain portion of this wealth paid for diverse supplies obtained in trade with Muslim merchants, mostly Turko-Iranian, though perhaps some Chinese too.

Securing a Rear Flank: The Tanguts Neutralized

In the years immediately after 1206, Chinggis did not send a delegation to the Tanguts inviting submission; the Mongols must have had good reasons for not making a friendly overture to the Xia ruler. Unlike other groups they had so far incorporated, the Tanguts were neither Turks nor nomads, although their population included both. Xia was a sedentary state governed by a Buddhist Sino-Tibetan-speaking elite; it paid nominal allegiance to Jin. The Kereyit ruling elite had cultivated connections among Xia aristocrats, especially in military circles, during various stints of exile there, and these ties may have predisposed some elements in the ruling strata against the Mongols.

Moreover, the Tanguts' roughly two-hundred-year history celebrated successful armed struggles to remain independent of Song, Liao, and Jin efforts to absorb or reduce them. Rashid al-Din's description of the Tanguts in his section on the "Turk tribes" (that they were not actually Turks is irrelevant here) makes it clear that they were later remembered chiefly for their mighty army, bellicose resistance to the Mongols, and mutinous posture. Whether or not such a reputation also preceded them is hard to say, but by 1207 Chinggis Khan surely had good sources of information on the Tanguts, including several defectors, and may have been advised that they would never acknowledge Mongol suzerainty without a fight. In fact, the appearance of the Mongols stirred up a hornet's nest for this proud people, as it did for others, and their inconsistent stance toward the new steppe power gave public face to the deadly factional strife that this development triggered or, given our almost complete lack of sources for contemporary Tangut politics, fed on.

So late in the autumn of 1207 Chinggis Khan led an attack on the Xia northern frontier outpost of Wulahai, on the edge of the Gobi near Önggüt territory and the Jin frontier, and returned north with a herd of camels in the spring of 1208. This sortie came at a critical juncture in relations among the three states occupying present-day China: Xia, Jin, and Song. Song, from the south, had just provoked a brief and disastrous war against Jin in 1206, at a time when the Jurchens were losing control over their northwestern frontier and suffering a series of bad harvests brought on by flood and draught. Their chief border ally, the Önggüts, openly defected to the Mongols in 1207, after the Jurchens had murdered Alakhush Digit Khuri in a vain attempt to pressure the Önggüt princes to remain loyal. Many of the mixed tribal groups employed by Jin to garrison its frontier resented being marshalled to fight against Song and likewise from 1207 on decamped to the Mongols. Now Jin faced a growing Mongol threat, an unguarded border to its rear, and severe food shortages.

The Mongol attack on Wulahai in 1207 widened the breach in the Jin frontier and probed Tangut defenses in the Ordos (the desert–steppe region within the northern loop of the Yellow River), clearing the way for a future attack on north China. But Wulahai was a well-fortified garrison, and the Mongols had no experience yet in taking walled settlements. Thus they returned in 1209, perhaps too because they discovered that the Tanguts had failed to secure Jin aid against them.

Following the Mongol withdrawal in the spring of 1208, the Xia court at Zhongxing dispatched a series of delegations throughout the year to the Jin court, some no doubt occasioned by the military emergency on their shared northern border. Despite Tangut efforts to gain Jin cooperation in meeting the crisis, none ensued. A tradition difficult to credit but widely repeated in Chinese sources places in the mouth of the Jin emperor (or his less capable successor, at the end of 1208) these apocryphal words: "It is to Our advantage when Our enemies attack each other. Wherein lies the danger to Us?" From then on Tangut–Jin relations soured and, to the Mongols' good fortune, they fell to attacking each other, which encouraged pro-Mongol sentiment at the Tangut court.

Chinggis Khan again led the Xia campaign of 1209, probably soon after the return of his first embassy to the Uighurs, whose domain lay west across the desert from Xia. Tangut relations with those Uighurs included trade and diplomatic and cultural exchanges; many other Uighurs lived in western Xia, served in the Xia government, or traveled frequently to and fro. The Xia state also cultivated good relations with Qara Khitai, by and large, and would not have wanted to jeopardize them by abetting the Uighurs' provocative insubordination. It must have pleased Chinggis to discover that the Uighurs needed him more at that moment than they valued relations with their eastern neighbors. He could lead his thousands back to Hexi without fear of interference.

The Tanguts were expecting them, for a Xia army met the advancing Mongol force west of Wulahai and north of the mountains guarding the approach to the Tangut capital. Defeating this army and taking its deputy commander as prisoner, the Mongols advanced on to Wulahai, surrounded the garrison, and took control of it after the defending general committed suicide rather than surrender. Taking with them a Xia official, the Mongols advanced through the Alashan Mountains toward the Tangut capital of Zhongxing (the present-day site of Yinchuan, capital of the Ningxia Hui Autonomous Region). After overcoming another Xia army and imprisoning the Tangut prince who led it, they surrounded Zhongxing.

Unfamiliar as yet with sedentary siege techniques and unable to breach the defenses of such a well-fortified city, the Mongols instead resorted to an ancient ruse by diverting the waters in the Yellow River canals nearby to flood the city. The canal dikes broke, however, flooding their own camps in the cold of approaching winter, so they had little choice but to halt the operation and withdraw. Before doing so they sent their Wulahai captive into the city to negotiate. The Tangut emperor agreed to tender allegiance to Chinggis Khan and hand over a daughter for the khan along with a substantial quantity of livestock and precious goods. Satisfied, the invading army returned to Mongolia early in 1210.

The *Secret History* account of the Tangut surrender is not prefaced with an account of the bungled military action that induced it (Chinese sources supply that information), perhaps a deliberate omission. Rather, in the Mongol saga the Tangut ruler is called "Burkhan khan," combining the Uighur word for "Buddha" (*Burkhan*) with the steppe royal title, alluding to the reputation of the Tangut monarchs as Buddhist kings. Burkhan khan offers his submission and promises, "[w]e shall become your right wing and we shall serve you." But then he qualifies the nature of their service. Because the Tanguts are a people who live in permanent camps and walled towns, when the Mongols go to combat,

> We shall not be able to hasten into a swift campaign, we shall not be able to fight a deadly combat. But if Chinggis Khan shows favor to us, we the Tangut people... shall bring forth many camels... and we shall give them to you. We shall weave woollen material and make satin, and we shall give them to you. Training falcons to fly loose at game, we shall gather them and all the best ones we shall send to you.

Here we have a clear statement that the Tanguts intended to provide supplies rather than manpower (they did send troops in 1216 and in 1221, but soon withdrew them), voicing a determination to preserve some autonomy. As we have seen, the Tanguts were not alone in attempting to have their cake and eat it too, but as the people in whose final conquest Chinggis Khan died, their valor is recognized in the *Secret History*. Also as the Mongols were in no position in the winter of 1209–1210 to argue over the intent behind Burkhan's words, they withdrew. It sufficed that Wulaihai now lay within the Mongol orbit. Rashid al-Din reports that Chinggis Khan left a garrison of Mongol troops there; around the same time he established a garrison in the Uighur realm. The Mongols' rear flank was now secure.

Into China: The First Jin Campaigns

Back in Mongolia from the Tangut campaign and briefed on Jurchen domestic difficulties and efforts to rebuild their border defenses, Chinggis Khan formally severed tributary relations with the Jin court later in 1210. According to the Chinese annals of the Yuan dynasty, the khan despised the new Jin emperor for his arrogance toward Chinggis when as a prince he (the new emperor) had received the Mongol chief's periodic tribute offerings. The real motive for attacking the Jin was, undoubtedly, the promise of plunder. In preparation, the Mongol khan convoked a *khuriltai* in the spring of 1211 to plan the impending campaign. Leaving behind twenty thousand troops under a trusted commander to forestall any act of dissidence among his new subjects, Chinggis Khan embarked on his first foray into north China. Rashid al-Din tells us that before setting out, the khan rode his horse up to the top of a mountain where he dismounted, removed his belt and slung it over his neck, and prayed for Heaven's blessing against the Altan Khan (Jin emperor), who had humiliated and tormented his ancestors. By some accounts, he spent three days on the mountain, in a prebattle ritual retreat. Justified and protected by Tengri, the Mongol khan set out against north China (see Map 7.1).

In the spring of 1211 the khan's army moved down from his *ordo* near the Kerulen River (by then a much larger camp city), with Mukhali commanding the Left Wing and his sons the Right Wing, and marched to the southern Gobi, their first base of operations against Jin. From there the Mongols launched several successful strikes against Jin fortifications, culminating in the seizure of the strategic pass at Juyongguan, which guarded the rugged northwest access to the main Jin capital at Zhongdu (near present-day Beijing). Some Mongol contingents penetrated and plundered the capital environs; others ravaged the Shanxi countryside. They withdrew north early in 1212, possibly because Chinggis suffered an arrow wound, to summer in Mongolia, taking with them booty and better knowledge of the enemy.

Meanwhile Khasar and Jebe, with Sübetei under him, led separate forays east into Manchuria as far as the Liao River valley, and early in 1213 temporarily occupied the Jin eastern capital (Dongjing, the city of Liaoyang). From the Yalu River valley bordering present-day Korea north to the maritime province of today's Russia, the forested hills of eastern Manchuria were the Jurchens' homeland. A century earlier, an ambitious Jurchen clan had united the other tribes under it to challenge and replace their nominal overlords, the Khitan Liao, whose homeland lay in western Manchuria and who, for two centuries, had ruled north Asia and a northern fringe of China down to present-day Beijing. The Jurchens went on to conquer all of north China and rule it as the Jin dynasty (1127–1234). The impending loss of Manchuria to the Mongols and the Jurchens' retreat south portended the end of their first dynasty in China. Four centuries later, they would rename themselves Manchus and return to Beijing, more experienced and better organized.

Map 7.1   North China, 1206–1227

In the autumn of 1212, after replenishing their herds, Chinggis Khan renewed the Jin campaign. Mongol troops had to recapture all the frontier posts attacked the year before and breached the pass at Juyongguan again only early in 1213. This time they advanced farther south in three main thrusts to spread out across the Jin heartland north of the Yellow River, ravaging, looting, and slaughtering the inhabitants of villages and towns across the plains of Shandong (east), Hebei (center), and Shanxi (west). They stationed garrison troops at all the main frontier passes to prevent them from slipping back into Jurchen control, and imposed a blockade on the capital at Zhongdu in the winter of 1213.

Although limited knowledge of siege warfare and susceptibility over the winter to human and livestock epidemics greatly hampered the Mongol siege, things were not much better at the Jin court, where chaos reigned. A new emperor, recently enthroned in a coup, panicked and offered terms. The Mongols accepted a rich tribute of silks, gold, silver, horses, and an imperial princess for Chinggis, in exchange for lifting the blockade in early spring of 1214. The princess was not the emperor's own daughter, but a daughter of the murdered Weishao Prince (his title of emperor retracted posthumously) whom Chinggis had so scorned. Nevertheless, she occupied an honored position in the ranks of the first five wives, though she bore no children to the Mongol khan.

Chinggis Khan's army returned to his campaign base in the Gobi, after dispatching several generals to conquer the territories east and west of the Liao River basin in Manchuria. By some accounts his agreement with the Jin emperor included returning all territories seized by the Mongols, but this part of the bargain never materialized. Terrified, the Jurchen court abandoned Zhongdu late in June and retreated south to their southern capital at Bianliang (Kaifeng, the old Song capital on the south bank of the Yellow River), where the arable land yielded more reliable food supplies.

When Chinggis got wind of this move, he at once ordered his officers back to Zhongdu; the remaining inhabitants put up a heroic resistance. It appears that by that time (late in 1214) much of the invaders' fighting was being done by local Khitan and Chinese recruits to the Mongol armies. The Jurchens also had to rely on the numerically superior local population, which undermined their defense operations beyond the capital. Chinggis resumed personal control of the Zhongdu blockade early in 1215, and the city surrendered in May of that year. The khan did not enter the city, which his troops looted and burned for a month.

In the *Secret History*, the Jurchen commander who surrendered the city greeted the Mongol deputies bearing gifts of precious satins. Shigi-khutukhu, the khan's first adopted son, warned his two colleagues against accepting goods that belonged rightfully to their master, for they had come to take an inventory of the "gold, silver, goods, satin and other things" collected in the general looting. Chinggis later "mightily rebuked" the two officers and praised Shigi-khutukhu for being "mindful of the great norm concerning one's obligation to the khan," that is, for his incorruptibility. This account emphasizes the steppe point of view, which focused on accountability for the plunder gained from raiding north China and its eventual circulation through proper channels. Concern for ravaged lands did not figure in the khan's calculations, though they may have in those of his increasingly numerous non-Mongol officers. In other words, to the extent that Chinggis Khan's campaigns of booty extraction in north China succeeded, they did so with the growing assistance of local recruits, who had a vested interest in repairing the damage done by troops fighting under the invaders' command. Eventually this investment would move the Mongols into making a longer-term commitment to their conquered territories than Chinggis had originally envisioned.

Mongol troops under Mukhali also reoccupied the Jin eastern capital in Manchuria and subjugated the region with Chinese and Khitan assistance. Khitan rebels in Mongol service turned the city into their base. When the Song court refused to submit the tribute payments agreed upon in the treaty ending the war they had instigated with Jin in 1206–1208, the Jin state teetered on bankruptcy. Anarchy and rebel movements sprouted on the heels of invasion and administrative breakdown. Chinese and Khitans defected to the rebels or powerful Mongol commanders. North China fell under the sway of Mongol generals and their local allies, or the various rebel organizations, some acting in concert with the Mongols. Another twenty years would pass, however, before the Jin state disappeared, owing to the conquerors' other preoccupations.

These were terrible years for the inhabitants of north China. The Mongols had no experience of governing sedentary peoples and cities, and little initial inclination to do so. Acknowledging this deficit early on, they recruited specialists who had such skills. Many Jin defectors (Jurchens, Chinese, and Khitans) accepted office or title under the Mongol commanders operating in north China, and through them the Mongols began to adapt Jin institutions to create some administrative structures for the conquered regions, primarily to extract local resources. The most prominent of these was the "branch secretariat" (*xing sheng*), a Jin regional office duplicating the functions of a central bureau located in the capital. This office became the forerunner of the modern Chinese province. The first Mongol branch secretariat arose on former Jin territory in 1214, and others quickly followed, headed by Mongol, Khitan, and some Chinese officers, who enjoyed full discretionary powers and appropriate Mongol military rank. Their sons entered the *keshig* (imperial guard) as hostages and in time inherited their father's offices.

"Mongolization" of the branch secretariats turned large areas of north China into autonomous, hybrid zones whose inhabitants for years faced the recurring threats of warfare, hunger, disease, and incessant demands from their regional lords for troops and taxes (usually goods in kind) to prosecute the ongoing conquest of north China. Gaining exemptions from such exactions became a major preoccupation for educated Chinese, beginning notably with religious groups, the Buddhists and Daoists. We will return to the resulting competition for patronage under the Mongols in Chapter 8. For Chinggis, the chief purpose of solidifying Mongol hold on the north Chinese territories remained their exploitation to support Mongol trade and military operations outside China. Conquering and governing China fell to his descendants.

Muhammad Shah's Mistake

By the spring of 1216 Chinggis Khan had moved back north to his *ordo* between the Kerulen and Tula rivers in central Mongolia. He had turned his attention to events developing out in central Asia and, needing his main army, left operations in north China under the command of Mukhali, upon whom he bestowed the hereditary title of *Prince of State* (*gui-ong* > Chinese *guo wang*) in 1217. Mukhali's Left Wing troops included twenty-three thousand of his own men plus perhaps double that number of Chinese and Khitan recruits. Their total strength is unclear; Rashid al-din gives an undated figure of sixty-two thousand. Mukhali had orders to pressure the Jin emperor to surrender most of north China and abdicate, to reign instead as the king of Henan (the southern-most Jin province).

In central Asia, meanwhile, two rival princes fought over the corpse of the dying Qara Khitai Empire: the Naiman refugee Küchlüg and the Turkic sultan 'Ala al-Din Muhammad (r. 1200–1220), ruler of Khwarazm, a rich Iranian trade emporium south of the Aral Sea. Küchlüg had wormed his way into the Qara Khitai ruling family by marrying a daughter of the gürkhan and converting to Buddhism, the royal clan's faith; he then took over the throne in 1211, assisted by another refugee from Mongolia, the Merkit prince, Khudu, and by the army of the *Khwarazm-shah* (the Iranian title used by the Turkic lords of this realm). For years the shah had been trying to reduce Qara Khitai dominion. With a force assembled from fellow Naiman and other tribal refugees, Küchlüg then turned on Muhammad and asserted control over Muslim territories that the sultan coveted. His policies cruelly oppressed Muslims and inflamed the local peoples. Moreover, he added insult to injury by killing a Qarluq chief who was enrolled as a vassal of Chinggis Khan and married to a Mongol princess.

The timing of the Mongol suppression of Küchlüg is confused and possibly conflated with other events, but most accounts have Chinggis dispatching his top generals in 1216 to deal with the Merkit and Naiman menace. Jochi and Sübetei set out to track the Merkit remnants under Khudu in the steppes west of Lake Balkash. After vanquishing a combined Merkit–Qangli force, they chased Khudu into the Qipchaq steppe and finally finished him off. Returning, they ran into the army of the Khwarazm-shah, staking his claim to the Qara Khitai western terri-tories. At this point accounts vary as to whether the Mongols actually clashed with the shah's army. On the one hand, probably Chinggis Khan did not want to provoke this western potentate, and therefore Jochi's troops employed the old trick of feigning a vast force by lighting many fires, then slipping off in the night to return east. Their orders from Chinggis did not include fighting with Muhammad. On the other hand, perhaps the two armies did clash, and Muhammad came away with a bitter taste in his mouth.

Jochi then headed off to southern Siberia to put down a rebellion of Forest Peoples that had erupted in 1217. Sübetei rejoined Jebe in the hunt for Küchlüg. From the central Asian oasis towns of Khotan and Kashgar (now in the People's Republic of China), where local Muslims had suffered Küchlüg's persecution, the Mongol party hounded the pretender into a valley in mountainous Badakhshan, southwest of Kashgar in the high Pamirs (today's Tajikistan). Juvaini describes how the Mongols secured the help of local hunters to end Küchlüg's dramatic career:

> "These men," they said, are Küchlüg and his followers, who have escaped from our grasp. If you capture Küchlüg and deliver him to us, we shall ask nothing more of you." These men [the hunters] accordingly surrounded Küchlüg and his followers, took him prisoner and handed him over to the Mongols; who cut off his head and bore it away with them. The people of Badakhshan received endless booty in jewels and money.... And be it remarked that whoever molests the faith and the law of Mohammed never triumphs....

By most accounts this mission took place sometime between 1216 and 1218, or possibly earlier.

Meanwhile, Muhammad sent envoys to Chinggis Khan in 1215 or 1216; after hearing news of the fall of the Jin capital, he wanted to learn more about his supposed rival in the conquest of China, an extravagant ambition attached to him by unflattering Muslim historians. Pleased, Chinggis cordially received the delegation and returned an embassy instructed to develop trade relations and solicit Mohammad's cooperation as an ally if not a vassal (the phrasing of his message has come down to us in many versions). "For in those days," Juvaini intones ominously, "the Mongols regarded the Moslems with the eye of respect, and for their dignity and comfort would erect them clean tents of white felt. . . ."

The Mongols' perennial interest in trade is echoed in many sources; Juvaini reports that the khan "posted guards (whom they called *qaraqchis*) upon the highways and issued a *yasa* that whatever merchants arrived in his territory should be granted safe conduct, while whatever merchandise was worthy of the Khan's acceptance should be sent to him together with the owner." His embassy to Muhammad arrived in 1218; it included a Khwarazmian merchant named Mahmud Yalavic (*Yalavic* means "messenger" in Turkic), who may have been a vizier to the last Qara Khitai ruler and thus would have offered his services to Chinggis Khan sometime after 1211. Yalavic later became the governor of the conquered areas of Turkestan. On this early mission, he tried to assuage the sultan's concerns. Suspicious of Mongol intentions, irritated that a fellow Khwarazmian preferred Chinggis Khan to himself, and evidently intent upon doing away with the upstart khan at some point, Muhammad nevertheless accepted the peace overture.

Subsequently, in 1218 the Mongols also outfitted a commercial entourage to escort some Khwarazmian merchants back home. According to Juvaini (who, while not always accurate in number or date, provides plausible details),

> Chingiz-Khan ordered his sons, *noyans* and commanders to equip, each of them, two or three persons from their dependents and give them capital of a *balish* [ingot] of gold or silver, that they might proceed with this party to the Sultan's territory, engage in commerce there and so acquire strange and precious wares.

Muslim merchants and the Mongols clearly perceived the advantages of mutual cooperation, all the more so then because the latter had ready access to Chinese manufactures in the form of loot and levies from north China. Chinggis Khan found merchants useful in diplomatic and commercial ventures; a Khwarazmian merchant named Jafar, who had taken the Baljuna oath with him in the dark days of 1203, negotiated the first Jin surrender of 1214 and became the first governor (*darughachi*) of the conquered land. Everyone understood that merchants spied as they bargained, and spread, as well as gathered, information. Merchants from Chinggis Khan might understandably have assumed airs as they recounted the feats of their patron.

The fateful trade caravan from the Mongols probably numbered about one hundred merchants, most Muslims. When it reached the Khwarazmian city of Otrar on the upper Syr Darya (which flows west into the Aral Sea, see Map 8.1), the local governor arrested the lot and sent a messenger to Muhammad. Whether on Muhammad's command or merely with the sultan's approval, he had the entire entourage (but one) killed and its goods confiscated. "Without pausing to think," Juvaini writes, "the Sultan sanctioned the shedding of their blood and deemed the seizure of their goods to be lawful, not knowing that his own life would become unlawful, nay a crime, and that the bird of his prosperity would be lopped of feather and wing." One man apparently escaped and conveyed the news of this evil event to the khan. This was a rash act, indeed, at a time when steppe etiquette entitled merchants to the same immunity and hospitality as diplomats. Then as now, killing an ambassador constituted an act of war. Outraged, Chinggis rushed an envoy to Muhammad demanding immediate retribution and restoration of the seized merchandise. Recklessly, Muhammad put the envoy to death. Juvaini describes Chinggis Khan's response to this news thus:

> Those tidings had such as effect upon the Khan's mind that the control of repose and tranquility was removed, and the whirlwind of anger cast dust into the eyes of patience and clemency while the fire of wrath flared up with such a flame that it drove the water from his eyes and could be quenched only by the shedding of blood. In this fever Chingiz-Khan went up alone to the summit of a hill, bared his head, turned his face towards the earth and for three days and nights offered up prayer, saying, "I was not the author of this trouble; grant me the strength to exact vengeance."

As for the foolish governor, in Juvaini's words, "nay rather he desolated and laid waste a whole world and rendered a whole creation without home, property or leaders."

Though conflict between two such ambitious warriors as Muhammad and Chinggis may have been inevitable, as many have argued, it was not a contest of equals. Brash and imprudent, Muhammad wielded only slender control over his own people and soldiers. Precipitating war with the Mongols exposed the Muslim world to an onslaught of seemingly unprecedented and unimaginable dimensions, endlessly embroidered in the laments of later Muslim chroniclers dutifully serving under their Mongol khans.

Family Business

On some occasion before departing Mongolia the following year to settle scores with Muhammad, Chinggis settled a critical item of family business. At the suggestion of his Tatar wife, Yisüi Khatun, the aging khan (now approaching sixty years) gathered his adult sons to designate a successor and obtain their promise to support the chosen one. It was at this all-important family council that his second son Chaghatai launched into his famous diatribe against elder son Jochi, the "Merkit bastard"; third son Ögedei emerged as the compromise candidate. This episode is related only, and at great length, in the *Secret History*, where its dramatic potential finds full exposition. When the father turns to his third son and asks, "Ögedei, what do you say? Speak up!" the latter replies, "When my father the Khan, favoring me, tells me to speak, what am I to say? I shall say that I will certainly try according to my ability." At the end of the discussion, Chinggis speculates on the future:

> Supposing that the descendants of Ögedei are all born so worthless that
> even if one wrapped them in fresh grass,
> they would not be eaten by an ox;
> even if one wrapped them in fat,
> they would not be eaten by a dog,
> is it possible that among my descendants not even a single one will be born who
> is good?

This ambiguous passage may be a later insertion by partisans of the factions that formed around the sons of Chinggis's sons in the succession wars and intrigues of the 1240s and 1250s. It would seem to justify either the claims of Ögedei's descendants to continue to hold the position of great khan, or the claims of other lines, specifically younger son Tolui's, to wrest the khanship away from Ögedei's successors. Undoubtedly Yisüi Khatun was not alone among Mongol women who could envision the scope of future family squabbling.

Jochi's alienation from the Golden Lineage's line of succession was mirrored in the physical distance separating his inheritance—a vast territory stretching from Lake Balkhash in central Asia south to Khwarazm, west to the frontier of eastern Europe and north to the Arctic Ocean (encompassing all of the Rus' lands; the Kazakh, Caspian, and Black sea steppes; and western Siberia)—from the Mongolian heartland. Eldest sons of nomads often moved far away when they came of age, and none more so than Jochi. His descendants devoted themselves to protecting the patrimony, often in conflict with neighboring Mongol-ruled Iran. Chapter 8 will explain how those territories came within the Mongols' orbit.

8

To Central Asia and Beyond: From Mongol Khan to World Conqueror, 1218–1223

How can my 'golden halter' be broken by the *Sarta'ul people? I shall set out against the Sarta'ul people.

—THE SECRET HISTORY OF THE MONGOLS

Punishing the Khwarazm-shah's crime required careful planning, and some of this took place at a *khuriltai* convoked toward the end of 1218. By then Chinggis Khan had news of Küchlüg's demise, and the former Qara Khitai lands abutting the Khwarazm-shah's realm lay secure in Mongol hands. While waiting for Jochi to subdue the rebellion of his discontented subjects in the northern forests around Baikal, Chinggis Khan recalled his Center and Right Wing armies for the new campaign, and left north China in Mukhali's capable hands.

Mukhali's Left Wing troops had gathered reinforcements from many newly absorbed Jurchen, Chinese, and Khitan troops. With his headquarters at Zhongdu, the former Jin capital, Mukhali assigned oversight of conquered territories to his recently enrolled Chinese officers, and opened a new front in Shanxi, northwest China. Throughout the next several years, while Chinggis Khan was campaigning in central and south Asia, Mukhali's forces slowly extended Mongol control and closed in on the Jin court at Bianliang, their southern capital. The Jurchens launched feckless offenses against the Song (which sent envoys to Mukhali in 1221 to explore an alliance against Jin), tried to counter Mongol thrusts, and continued to rebuff the Xia until 1225. They dispatched envoys to negotiate with Chinggis, but found Mongol peace terms unacceptable. Mukhali's death in the spring of 1223, however, interrupted a difficult campaign to take key well-fortified cities (Chang'an and Fengxiang) and gave the Jin a breathing space. While Chinggis Khan dealt with other pressing matters, operations in north China ground to a halt and resumed only after the khan's death in 1227 and the enthronement of his successor in 1229.

When Chinggis Khan's army headed southwestward into central Asia, two notable figures went along as members of his advisory staff. One was Mahmud Yalavic, the Khwarazmian member of the diplomatic mission to Samarqand in

---

*Sarta'ul (Sartagh) was the Mongol term for any central or western Asian Muslim.

1218. The other was Yelü Chucai, a highly literate and multilingual Khitan from the former Jin capital. These men later assumed responsibility for administering conquered areas in Turkestan and north China, respectively. Yelü Chucai, a tall man with a long beard (dubbed Urtu Sakhal, "Long Beard," by Chinggis), afterward composed an account of his travels during the Western Campaign, the manuscript of which was discovered in Japan only ca. 1926. His writings shed light on the sectarian factionalism that the conquest conditions created in north China among Daoists and Buddhists competing for protection under the Mongol umbrella. Yelü Chucai, himself a Buddhist, passed more than a year in Samarqand, the center of Mongol operations in central Asia. Chinggis Khan consulted him frequently owing to his gift for prognoses, by which Chucai gained authority, one of his predictions being the successful conquest of Khwarazm.

In the spring of 1219 Chinggis Khan summoned his armies, augmented by Chinese, Khitan, and other units from conquered or surrendered peoples, and set out from his home camp on the Kerulen. The khan's younger brother stayed behind with most of the family to guard the "hearth." Eldest son Jochi, just returned from quelling rebellion in south Siberia, along with his other sons Tolui, Chaghadai, and Ögedei accompanied the Western expeditionary armies. Jebe and Sübetei led the khan's vanguard. These forces assembled in the steppe along the Irtysh River, and in late summer moved south into central Asia. Reaching Qayaliq, on the lower Chu River, Chinggis Khan welcomed his Qarluq and Uighur vassal princes with their contingents. The combined army now numbered some one hundred and fifty thousand to two hundred thousand men. Chinggis led the main force toward Khwarazm's principal urban centers in Transoxania, between the rivers Syr Darya and Amu Darya, home of a flourishing Turko-Iranian Muslim culture (see Map 8.1).

The Khwarazm-Shah's Realm

The urban oases in the deserts and mountains of southwest Asia between the Caspian and Aral seas, supported by a flourishing irrigated agriculture, produced a civilization unfamiliar to the Mongols, though not to their Turk allies. In this frontier between the northern steppes and the Arabo-Persian civilization to the southwest, Islamicized Turks made their living as intermediaries, warriors, traders, and sultans. Khwarazm blended Turkic and Iranian influences; peasants and merchants were usually Persian in origin, rulers and soldiers being Turk. Linguistic Turkicization proceeded rapidly from the eleventh century to the thirteenth century. Transoxania (the land between the Amu Darya and Syr Darya rivers) had come under the Khwarazm-shah's dominion only a few years before the Mongol invasion, and its people felt no special allegiance to their new overlord.

Khwarazm-shah Muhammad ('Ala al-Din Muhammad, II) was descended from a Turk military slave who rose to power as a regional governor of the Seljuk rulers (also Turks) of Persia. His mother, Terken-khatun, was the daughter of a Qangli–Qipchaq chief, a subgroup of the Turks who were nomadizing across the Kazakh and Pontic steppes. Muslim writers of the thirteenth century refer to the vast plain north of Lake Balkhash and the Aral, Caspian, and Black seas as the

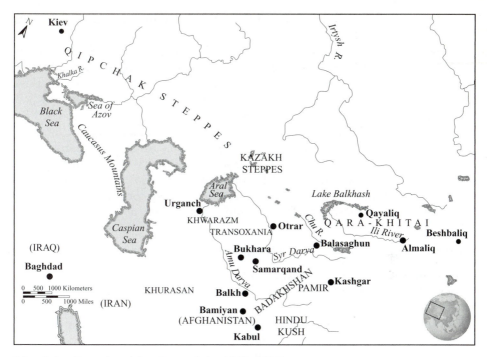

Map 8.1 Central and Southwest Asia, 1200–1227

Qipchaq steppe (Desht-i Qipchaq). Close ties with the Qipchaqs, usually through marriage alliances, supplied the armies of aspiring regional rulers in their struggles with other local powers to take over Transoxania. By 1209 Muhammad had enlarged his Khwarazmian core, whose chief city was Urganch, with the Persian territory of Khurasan to the southwest, much of Afghanistan to the south and southeast, and Transoxania, but he had yet to consolidate his rule over this motley empire. To exacerbate matters, Terken-khatun wielded more power and influence than he did, especially over the Qipchaq troops in his army. Muhammad enjoyed nothing like the loyalty that Chinggis Khan commanded of his warriors.

The Khwarazm-shah chose to meet the Mongol advance by dividing up his army into units of twenty thousand to fifty thousand dispatched to defend the various cities in his realm, leaving one hundred and ten thousand men in the regional capital of Samarqand. He did not take to the field in person, nor did he allow his spirited son, Jalal al-Din, to do so. Rather, he withdrew to the west; he ran away. Muhammad was not particularly liked by, nor did he trust, his Turk generals. He calculated that he would be safer giving them troops to defend their cities than allowing them to take command of a large army in the field. But forcing the Mongols to engage in long, drawn-out sieges of each city they approached, instead of weakening or dispersing them in pitched battle out in open country, prolonged and indirectly contributed to the slaughter and bloodshed that popular resistance inevitably provoked. Jalal al-Din condemned his father's cowardly strategy; the Muslim historians universally castigate Muhammad's tactics and failure of nerve. It is no surprise that Khwarazm fell to the Mongols in less than two years.

Otrar, site of the original offense, was the Mongols' first target in early fall of 1219. To protect their rear, Jochi led an army out into the steppes north of the Syr Darya against the nomadic Qangli and Qipchaq allies of Muhammad, then pressed on to other centers down toward the mouth of the river. Chinggis Khan put Chaghadai and Ögedei in charge of operations at Otrar and proceeded on across the desert to Bukhara, saving the bastion of Samarqand for later, to increase pressure on the city and clear the countryside around it. These Mongol forces featured more than mounted archers; in contrast to the early campaigns against Xia, in 1219 Chinese and Muslim experts in siege craft—chemical and engineering technologies to penetrate and reduce heavy fortifications—formed special regiments in each army. Walls would not stop them now.

Mongol Military Operations from Otrar to Samarqand

A five-month siege of Otrar ensued. The governor (whose earlier actions had caused the crisis) blocked all attempts by his subordinates to surrender. A defending general who slipped out was caught and executed by the Mongols for disloyalty to his master. Entering the city, the invaders emptied it of commoners and looted it, then fought for another bloody month with the remaining troops holed up in the citadel. After much loss of life, they captured the governor, bound him in chains to deliver later to Chinggis Khan at Samarqand, and departed, herding the survivors before them. In the course of gathering booty, the Mongols razed the citadel and city walls to broaden passage for horses. Artisans and women were valued and spared; young men were made to march in the front lines to absorb assaults and shield the army.

Military prowess alone did not win Khwarazm for the invaders. Mongol strategy emphasized efficiency and made use of any means available to achieve a goal with the fewest casualties to men and animals. Nothing enraged Chinggis Khan and elicited Mongol wrath more than the loss of good warriors to intransigence. Thus they avoided pitched battle whenever possible, engaged in strategic retreat or withdrawal when the odds did not favor them, and relied heavily on ruse and psychological manipulation. Typically they combined exhortations to surrender with calculated terror and destruction. When a populace surrendered, the Mongols herded them out of the town walls; looted the place; razed any fortifications; and departed with booty and choice slaves, to be turned over to the khan's treasury or distributed among the Mongol princes at the khan's discretion.

The Mongols deployed defectors to spread rumors and disinformation; Chinggis Khan adroitly exploited tensions among the Khwarazmian ruling nobles, particularly between Muhammad and his mother, to undermine their unity. In addition, standard procedure dictated that a Khwarazmian in Mongol service address the inhabitants upon arrival at each city, advising against resistance. Juvaini writes that at the first town on the road to Bukhara, for example, the populace listened to Chinggis Khan's messenger and "turn[ing] their faces toward the path of advantage" were spared, except for the young men drafted into the frontlines of the army. Many other small towns followed suit.

Chinggis reached Bukhara, a major cultural center, in February 1220 and pitched camp in front of the city walls. There popular resentment against the ruling elite for turning the city over to Muhammad in 1207 played into Mongol hands. Thinking to save themselves, the city's commanders snuck out at night, only to be captured and slain by Mongol troops. The main garrison dispersed or met a similar fate. A few hundred Turk troops retreated into the citadel to resist. The next morning the people opened the city gates and Chinggis Khan entered to receive their submission. Juvaini relates that following this meeting, Chinggis entered the town and approached the Friday mosque. Upon learning that it was not a palace but a "house of God," he mounted the pulpit and announced that the "countryside is empty of fodder; fill our horses' bellies." People quickly gathered all the grain and brought it into the courtyard of the mosque. "And they brought the cases in which the Korans were kept out into the courtyard of the mosque, where they cast the Korans right and left and turned the cases into mangers for their horses. After which they circulated cups of wine and sent for the singing-girls of the town to sing and dance for them; while the Mongols raised their voices to the tunes of their own songs." After this entertainment, Chinggis returned to his camp outside Bukhara; a respected imam explained to the horrified clerics attending these events: "Be silent: it is the wind of God's omnipotence that bloweth, and we have no power to speak."

As usual, the population had to evacuate while Mongol troops plundered the city's wealth and food stocks, in the course of which fires broke out and burned the town down. A fierce battle ensued to dislodge the Qangli soldiers from the citadel; none survived. All adult Qangli males perished, while the women and children were enslaved. Of the rest of the city dwellers, fit males became cannon fodder for the march against Samarqand, artisans entered Mongol service, and the rest fled to villages in the hinterland.

Samarqand, the jewel of Transoxania, lay east of Bukhara. In a popular revolt against the Khwarazm-shah in 1212, many residents had been killed; and when Muhammad retook the city, ten thousand more died. (Perhaps we should not take these figures too literally.) Now the sultan, his advisors, and his mother had all abandoned the city, leaving fifty thousand Tajik (Persian-speaking) troops and sixty thousand Turks to last out the siege. These numbers seem impossibly large, combined with the numerous civilian inhabitants upon whom the burden of the sultan's military forces lay. This burden, along with the news of Bukhara's fate, sowed doubt and dissension among Samarqand's populace on the wisdom of resistance, as the Mongols, reunified after the fall of Otrar, approached in March 1220. Chinggis Khan spent several days inspecting the walls and considering his options. Several more days of combat between the arrayed Mongol armies and the defenders, sallying forth on horseback or elephants to martyrdom (as the Persian historians put it), encouraged the townspeople to negotiate.

Chinggis Khan received a delegation from the city's merchant and clerical elite, offering surrender in exchange for protection. Samarqand thereupon opened its gates. Mongol soldiers drove most of the population out of the gates, and set to work sacking the city and leveling its walls and towers. A large group of evacuees under the protection of the clerics (some astounding fifty thousand) remained untouched, in accordance with the bargain struck with the Mongol khan. Those who tried to hide inside the city perished. The invaders assaulted the citadel and forced what remained of the garrison to pay the price of resistance, resulting in the reputed slaying of thirty thousand Qangli and other Turk soldiers. More than three hundred artisans and many women were apportioned among the Mongol nobility; a hefty monetary contribution was levied from the surviving population. Young men were corralled into the army as its human shield. The entire operation lasted about ten days.

From his camp outside Samarqand, Chinggis Khan dispatched generals to take other cities along the Syr Darya. He had learned that Muhammad had crossed the Amu Darya into Khurasan (northern Persia) and Iraq, south and west of Samarqand, leaving behind the bulk of his retinue and army in the various towns and villages. Thus the khan sent Jebe and Sübetei ahead with thirty thousand troops to track the sultan and his heir, while he himself moved southeast into the mountain valleys of the Hindu Kush along the present-day border of Uzbekistan and Afghanistan in the summer of 1220, to rest and replenish the horses and livestock that always accompanied the armies. In pursuit of their quarry, Jebe and Sübetei left behind *darughachis* or Mongol governors in those towns that surrendered to them and destroyed those that resisted.

In the autumn of 1220 Chinggis advanced southwest toward Balkh, stopping to pass the winter before crossing the Amu Darya into Khurasan. Suspicious of the potential resistance being organized by the sultan's charismatic son, Jalal al-Din, the khan's armies showed no mercy to the towns, even those offering to surrender, lying along the route followed by the fleeing ruler. In the spring of 1221, Balkh, which had earlier rebelled against its Mongol governor, surrendered again, but its people were all put to the sword. Many other towns resisted and met a similar end. At Bamiyan, luckless site of the ancient colossal Buddhist cave temples in Afghanistan, Chaghadai's son (the khan's favorite grandchild) commanded the operation and died in the resisters' fire. In revenge the Mongols obliterated the place and its inhabitants, decreed that no one should ever live there, and renamed it Bad Fortress. (The Buddhist remains at Bamiyan suffered Taliban ravages in more recent times.) Meanwhile, Chinggis Khan sent his youngest son Tolui on to conquer the other towns of Khurasan while his three elder sons marched on Urganch, Khwarazm's main commercial center, at the mouth of the Amu Darya.

The fall of Samarqand sealed the fate of Khwarazm. Sultan Muhammad's mother, Terken-khatun, had departed the oasis before the Mongols arrived and went first to Urganch. There she received a messenger from Chinggis Khan, offering her rule over her unworthy son's territories. A message from Muhammad, however, prompted her to abandon Urganch and take refuge in a stronghold south of the Caspian, after murdering many of her courtiers. Besieged and driven to extremity, Terken-khatun surrendered to Jebe and Sübetei several months later and was sent to Chinggis Khan. She ended her days a miserable prisoner in Mongolia; all of her grandsons were killed, and her son's daughters and harem distributed among the Mongol princes.

With Jebe and Sübetei hot on his heels, Muhammad retreated to an island in the south Caspian Sea, where he died of an illness at the end of 1220 or in January 1221. Muhammad's heir, Jalal al-Din, proved himself a worthier opponent to the Mongols. Chinggis Khan's army chased him endlessly up, down and across southwest Asia, but he always eluded them and even routed troops under chief judge Shigi-Khutukhu, the first defeat sustained outside of Mongolia. Only in 1231, well after Chinggis Khan had returned east and become an ancestor, did Jalal al-Din close a colorful career of celebrated exploits at the hands of unknowing Kurdish robbers.

Dozens of towns and cities fell to the Mongol armies in 1220 and 1221, following a fairly predictable pattern. Resisters, high officials or confidants of the Sultan Muhammad, and defiant garrison troops were uniformly massacred; artisans and women became slaves to be shipped off to headquarters and doled out as booty. Herat, like Balkh, had managed to secure a peaceful surrender in the spring of 1221, only to revolt again later in December, for which the town was annihilated. Only some one thousand weavers survived because earlier they had been transported north to Besh Baliq (in the Tianshan Mountains), for their skills in making gold brocade cloth. Later under Chinggis's successor, Ögedei (r. 1229–1241), Herat was rebuilt and some of the weavers returned home.

Thorough extraction of all portable wealth accompanied the leveling of walls, towers, and fortifications. Fire often destroyed what remained. In certain cases, the Mongols spared no one, although it is clear that some people escaped, later to return and repopulate the towns. Mongol commanders appointed a governor (*darughachi*) to remain in the towns with a small garrison to oversee the surviving population. However, not all enemy soldiers perished under Mongol swords; increasingly they entered the ranks of the Mongol armies. Many Mongol soldiers also died in these campaigns, and troop strength did not diminish, indicating a high rate of desertion among Turkic troops in the region.

The acquisition of such large quantities of slaves and wealth, as well as territory, in the course of the Western Campaigns exacerbated frictions among the khan's sons, in particular Jochi and Chaghadai. Conflict surfaced at the siege of Urganch on the south Aral coast in the fall of 1220, a joint operation of Jochi, Chaghadai, and Ögedei. As the encircling Mongol troops engaged in elaborate preparations, the populace united to resist. Evidently because Chinggis Khan had given the city to Jochi as part of his intended appanage, Jochi sought to stem the destruction (and thereby preserve its wealth) by repeatedly encouraging the people to surrender in exchange for protection. Chaghadai, a stern man who upheld his father's decrees to the letter, disparaged this self-indulgent posture toward the recalcitrant city dwellers.

The quarrel between Jochi and Chaghadai probably prolonged the seven-month siege and cost the invaders further casualties. When Mongol troops breached the walls, they had to engage in hand-to-hand combat through every street and quarter, tossing naphtha fire bombs as they went. Appalling slaughter and destruction ensued. Finally, in April 1221, they drove the remaining inhabitants out of the city, rounded up the skilled craftsmen, children, and young women, and slew the rest. Along the way, the river dikes collapsed, flooding much of the town.

When Chinggis Khan learned of discord at Urganch, he ordered Ögedei to take charge and demanded that his three sons appear before him at their earliest opportunity. He finally met with Chaghadai and Ögedei two years later, in the spring of 1223 on the route north toward his *ordo*. But Jochi never returned to Mongolia. The elder son remained in the west, consolidating his personal *ulus* or territorial domain. He refused his father's commands (or entreaties) to appear in person, greatly angering the khan. Jochi died before his father of unknown causes, almost certainly nonnatural. In time Urganch became an important Golden Horde commercial city, surpassing Chaghadaid-ruled Bukhara and Samarqand.

Pursuit of Muhammad and Jalal al-Din opened up new itineraries for the Mongol khan and his armies into Khurasan, Afghanistan, India, the Caucasus region (Georgia and Azerbaijan), and the Qipchaq steppes of southern Russia. By September 1221, Chinggis Khan had trapped Jalal al-Din on the banks of the Indus River (in present-day Pakistan). The sprightly sultan galloped into the water to cross the river, his eager enemies restrained from plunging in after him by an awed Chinggis who allegedly withdrew, Juvaini writes, repeating the words, "Such a son a father must have." As the year 1221 drew to a close, the khan, now close to sixty years old, marched up the Indus River to begin the long journey north to Mongolia, having received news of setbacks in north China and further Tangut perfidy. The khan had hoped to find a suitable route home through north India and the Himalayas, but the climate and terrain disagreed with the health of his men and mounts, and the omens were discouraging, so they turned back the way they had come.

Meanwhile Jebe and Sübetei had looped around the Caspian Sea up through the Caucasus region, attacked the Georgians twice, forced their way by ruse through a pass in the mountains on the west coast of the Caspian, and engaged various hostile tribes in battle, chiefly Alans and Qipchaqs. They probably spent the summer of 1222 pasturing their mounts in the lush steppes north of the Black and Caspian seas, before marching on to reconnoiter and engage the allied armies of the Qipchaq and Russian princes on the Khalka River (which flows into the Sea of Azov) in May 1223. After further scouting around in the Russian borderlands, they made their way east, meeting up with Chinggis Khan's army later in 1223 and arriving in Mongolia in 1224. From the information they provided, Chinggis Khan commanded Jochi (presumably by courier) to lead a campaign against the rulers of the Qipchaq steppe and add it to the empire. Jochi never got around to this task, and it fell to his son and successor Batu to carry out under a new great khan in the 1230s. These lands formed the core of the Golden Horde, or *ulus*, of Batu and his descendants.

Chinggis and the Daoist Adept

Both at his camp in the Hindu Kush in 1222 and back in Samarqand in 1222 and 1223, Chinggis Khan held a series of interviews with a renowned Chinese Daoist master named Changchun, whom he had summoned from north China to deliver up to him the secret of long life (and good government, according to the letter of invitation, though the khan as well as the master focused on the former). The invitation went out on the advice of a Chinese physician in the khan's retinue who claimed that the Daoist adept was three hundred years old and could prolong Chinggis's life. Changchun demurred and instead advised the khan to avoid women, the hunt, and alcohol. The khan acknowledged the soundness of this advice, though he could not promise to follow it, and showered the aged Daoist with gifts and privileges for his sect back in China.

A disciple in Changchun's entourage kept a diary of the three-year journey from north China to the Hindu Kush and back and the conversations that took place between his master and the khan, facilitated by the translations of a polylingual Tangut and the Khitan governor of Samarqand. He did not transcribe the philosophical themes expanded upon by the master, but one lecture was recorded by Yelü Chucai and published separately in 1232. Yelü Chucai, introduced earlier as a Khitan secretary and prognosticator to the khan, had composed the original invitation to the Daoist and was present in Samarqand during Changchun's sojourn. A devout syncretist in his own study of the Three Sages (Confucius, Buddha, and Laozi), Chucai at first thought highly of Changchun, because the Daoist's teaching also incorporated Confucian and Buddhist tenets; the aged adept might exert a beneficial influence on the aging khan. But if the goal in inviting Changchun was to bring the bloody campaigns to a halt, they failed.

According to Changchun's diarist, Chinggis delighted in the Daoist's discourses, often ordering them to be written down, and at least once summoning his sons and other notables to be edified, claiming that "Heaven sent this holy Immortal to tell me these things. Do you engrave them upon your heart." He approved the suggestion that the Mongols' taboo on washing in streams to avoid offending the water spirits was no way to serve Heaven. Rather they should avoid ill-treating their mothers and fathers. Later, after Chinggis escaped injury in a hunting accident, the sage suggested that to nurture himself in his advancing years the khan might cut back on hunting. The khan promised to heed this advice, and the diarist commented, "It was indeed two months before he again went hunting."

Perhaps more portentously, after long hours in Changchun's company Yelü Chucai grew disillusioned with the Daoist, whom he found ill-informed about Buddhism and concerned merely to convert people to his own weird brand of esoteric alchemy. How discouraging to see his Mongol master fawn over the man! After Changchun's return to China, tensions arose over the interpretation of a tax exemption granted by the khan to monastic institutions in north China. Changchun's followers claimed it applied only to them, and presumed upon their alleged imperial prerogatives to seize properties belonging to Confucians and Buddhists. After the deaths in 1227, of both Changchun and his patron, the Mongol khan, these hostilities erupted into bitter religious strife. The Buddhist–Daoist conflict that lasted decades in north China owed much to this singular episode in Chinggis's Western Campaign. Yelü Chucai published his travel account after returning to Yanjing (former Zhongdu/Beijing) in 1229, following the publication of the Daoist's diary; he hoped it would justify to the Daoists' victims his support for introducing Changchun to Chinggis Khan in the first place.

In the Aftermath of the Western Campaign

Among Juvaini's stories about the surrender of Bukhara is an incident illustrated in a Persian miniature painting at the British Library. Chinggis Khan lectures the city's elders, explaining to them that their sins had brought this disaster upon them: ". . . I am the punishment of God. If you had not committed great sins, God would not have sent a punishment like me upon you." In these words, as in those attributed by Juvaini to the respected imam of the city, we hear the human desire to explain the inexplicable. For Muslims, only the wrath of Allah, provoked beyond endurance by their sins (of which they readily admitted to the full gamut), could make sense of the Mongol cataclysm. Moreover, such a speech would be quite plausible within the framework of Mongol ideology, substituting "treachery" and "defiance" for "sins" and Tengri for God/Allah.

The various messengers sent by the Mongols to announce their arrival at each city touched on such themes as Chinggis Khan's appointment by Heaven to rule the world and punish evil doers (i.e., their rulers). Juvaini quotes a man who escaped to Khurasan and delivered this warning: "They came, they sapped, they burnt, they slew, they plundered, and they departed." The chronicler comments, "Men of understanding who heard this description were all agreed that in the Persian language there could be nothing more concise than this speech," alluding wryly to the ornamental style of literary composition, which favored extravagant and allusive metaphors over plain parts of speech.

The historiographical record gives unanimous voice to a cataclysm of monumental proportions. More difficult to accept are the numbers of people claimed to have been killed in Khwarazm and Persia; the immense figures often quoted in Muslim histories seem to convey more the enormity of the calamity, in the writers' eyes, than exact tallies of its toll. It is hardly likely that cities in Khurasan or Transoxania had populations of over several hundred thousand, much less a million or more (no matter how much the large garrisons and fleeing peasants inflated the figures). Although the conquests indeed devastated the region thoroughly, places said to have been obliterated had revived not many years later; rebellions occurred in some towns against their Mongol-appointed governors, indicating that some people were left to be governed and to rebel.

As modern authors have pointed out, the Mongols did not spread a uniform blanket of destruction; amid the wreckage lay large swathes of relatively untouched countryside. Northern Persia (Khurasan) suffered most, owing to the vulnerability of its ingenious irrigation system. Without peasants to maintain and repair the underground water channels, deserts reclaimed the fields, agriculture died out, and cities dwindled or disappeared. As great numbers of farmers perished or fled in the invasions of 1221–1223, and as the Mongols were still inclined to view pastures as more useful than farms, this did indeed occur to a great extent. Later Mongol governors, notably Mahmud Yalavic and his son, made efforts to repair the damage done to the sedentary economy of the empire during the early conquests, but Transoxania and Khurasan never completely recovered from the furious onslaught that the lust for vengeance brought down upon their peoples. Less personal, more political motives spurred the subsequent conquests of south China, Persia, Iraq, Russia, and other lands. After Chinggis Khan's death, his heirs, raised in a different world, devised grander designs for long-term occupation and adjusted their strategies accordingly.

In other words, we may understand the Mongol genocide inflicted upon this region as a confluence of several forces: (1) the cultural logic of revenge (they killed our envoys!); (2) an alien ecology (what use are farmers and fields?); (3) a limited agenda (punish and retreat); and (4) timing (the first big campaign far from home). To a large extent these factors also explain the destruction of north China in the first decades of Mongol campaigning in east Asia. There is another element: military leadership.

Contemporary and later writers, especially in the sedentary world, described the Turko-Mongols (or Tatars) with a horror verging on fascination as barbarians unleashing savagery and death, as the unpent minions of evil loosed on them by an angry deity. "Hordes" (from *ordo*, "palace encampment") and "Tartars" have become the sedentary shorthand for uncivilized, cruel, barbaric human beings. Yet the Mongols were probably no more savage in their conduct of war than armies through the ages; they *were* more successful, and on a much larger scale.

In explaining Mongol military successes, most writers point to the nomads' training from childhood on horseback with the bow, in the hunt; their pastoral culture (ecological adaptation), which encouraged hardiness, endurance, mobility, discipline, cooperative decision making, and above all adaptability to sudden changes in the environment; the outstanding commanders whom Chinggis Khan attracted to his cause and trusted with considerable battlefield autonomy; the reorganization of his armies, which diluted older tribal allegiances in favor of loyalty to the supreme commander; the iron discipline enforced upon them; and Chinggis's adroit political calculations.

Jebe, the legendary Sübetei, Mukhali, Bo'rochu, Khubilai, Jelme, and the other "heroes" were all men of skill, discipline, courage, dedication, ingenuity, fortitude, who ate the same food as their troops and shared the hardships of campaign. Yet more than fine strategy and leadership account for Mongol military success. Despite their limited agenda, the campaign required considerable behind-the-lines administration.

The Daoist sage Changchun spent several months in Samarqand shortly after its fall, over the winter of 1221 and summer and fall of 1222. His disciple's record of the journey opens a window on life in the wake of the Western Campaign. In the diary we catch glimpses of the infrastructure laid behind the frontlines to manage the flow of people and resources to and from east Asia and the camps of the "Golden Family" during these years: the poststations, military colonies with their multinational artisan and farming populations, newly erected roads and bridges, granaries and storehouses, escorts and interpreters, work crews and engineers. Changchun's party reached Samarqand after many months of travel on December 3, 1221. The honored visitors stopped to await spring and more favorable traveling conditions, affording the diarist ample opportunity for observation:

> Before the defeat of the Khwarizm Shah there was a fixed population here of more than 100,000 households; but now there is only about a quarter of this number, of whom a very large proportion are native Hui-ho [i.e., Central Asian Muslims]. But these people are quite unable to manage their fields and orchards for themselves, and are obliged to call in Chinese, Khitai [i.e., Khitan] and Tanguts. The administration of the town is also conducted by people of various nationality. Chinese craftsmen are found everywhere. Within the city is a mound about a hundred feet high on which stands the Khwarizm Shah's new palace. The Mongol governor at first resided there. But the local population was exasperated by famine and there was perpetual brigandage. Fearing trouble, the Governor went to live on the north side of the river. The Master [i.e., Changchun], however, consented to live in this palace. . . .

Refusing gifts of wine, Changchun asked instead for the local grapes to supply his steady stream of visitors, chiefly the resident Chinese brought in from north China. We learn that Muhammad's old palace still stood as well, for Changchun left a graffito in verse there. On a walk to the west side of the town, one fine day in early spring (probably with Yelü Chucai along), "wherever we went we came to terraces, lakes, pagodas and towers, with here and there an orchard or vegetable garden," confirming the contribution of imported east Asian labor to the revival of Samarqand.

For Changchun, the main difficulty in leaving the fertile oasis and proceeding south to Chinggis Khan's camp in Afghanistan was the scarcity of plant food south of the Amu Darya, for he was, of course, a vegetarian. Nonetheless, he set out in late April 1222 with a Mongol escort and in less than a month reached the khan's camp north of Kabul, just as warm weather was forcing it to relocate back into the Hindu Kush. The diarist observed that when his master had first arrived at the camp at the end of April, pastures and trees were all green and the herds nicely fattened, but when they left a month later, "there was no longer a blade of grass or any vegetation," pointing to a major logistical challenge of all Mongol military operations, not dissimilar to the Daoist's dietary dilemma: availability of pasture sufficient to nourish the Mongols' mounts and livestock (their walking larder). Typically, each soldier carried with him around five mounts (and no fewer than two), several servants, a cartload of weapons, and a small herd (30) of sheep and goats. Even if a chiliarch or "thousand" consisted of only seven hundred or five hundred men so equipped, it would require a huge acreage to sustain three or four chiliarchs en route to and during operations. Imagine thirty-five thousand horses and two hundred and ten thousand head of livestock, at a minimum, for a division of ten thousand.

On that account alone it was imperative for Mongol armies to split up into manageable, well-spaced units and move in separate directions. Considerable amounts of baggage would have to remain at a distant camp during a siege. According to many historians, the absence of adequate pasture accounts for the Mongol withdrawal from eastern Europe, Syria, India, and other places initially targeted for sustained assault. This simple fact of nomad life helps us understand better the early Mongol attitude toward tilled fields and walled cities enclosing narrow streets crammed with small houses. The incomprehension was mutual.

By the autumn of 1222 the armies under Chinggis Khan moved out of Afghanistan (the Hindu Kush) and, reuniting with the other Mongol forces in central Asia, returned to their staging camp on the Irtysh River in the summer of 1224. Chinggis Khan was back at his *ordo* in Mongolia the following spring, planning the Tangut campaign, his last.

9

Return to Mongolia: The Last Tangut Campaign and Chinggis Khan's Death, 1224–1227

I have conquered for you, my sons, a vast and far-flung empire that overshadows a year's distance in every direction. Now I charge you in repelling enemies and elevating friends to be of one mind and one face so that you may pass your days in comfort and enjoy kingship.

—RASHID AL-DIN, COMPENDIUM OF CHRONICLES

T he *Secret History* recounts that as Chinggis Khan was preparing for his Western Campaign, he sent envoys to request armed support from the Tangut king. Before the latter could respond, "Asha Gambu [a Xia courtier] forestalling him said, 'Since Chinggis Khan's forces are incapable of subjugating others, why did he go as far as becoming khan?' So saying, he did not dispatch auxiliary troops. . . ." When his envoys returned this message, Chinggis Khan determined to punish Tangut impudence once he had completed his business out in central Asia. From Chinese sources, we learn that a small contingent of Mongol troops surrounded the capital in 1217 or 1218 (the latter year more probably) after the Tangut ruler had departed to a southern city, leaving his son in charge. It seems he anticipated the Mongol demand, and fearing immediate reprisal for his court's refusal of aid, made a strategic retreat. Most likely the pro-Jin faction at the Xia court planned to take advantage of the khan's preoccupation in central Asia to repair relations with Jin and forge a united front against further Mongol aggression.

In this effort, the Tanguts made belated progress, but not soon enough. Whatever suspicions the Mongols harbored were confirmed by the events of 1222–23. Rashid al-Din and other Muslim historians mention news of a Tangut rebellion that Chinggis Khan received, which persuaded him to go home. Most likely this refers to a withdrawal late in 1222 of Tangut troops sent to support Mukhali's operation in Shaanxi, close to the Jin border with Xia. For this betrayal, which hinted at more ominous anti-Mongol schemes, Chinggis Khan authorized raids against Xia, led by Mukhali's son Bol and several of his Chinese commanders in the fall of 1224 (Mukhali died in 1223).

Tangut alienation threatened to undermine a larger Mongol objective, which had taken shape in 1221–1222. Diplomatic missions from the Song court in south China to both Chinggis Khan and Mukhali had proposed alliance with the Mongols against the Jin (on the theory, false as it so often turns out, that the enemies of one's enemy must be one's friend). A Jin peace mission arrived at Chinggis Khan's camp in northern Afghanistan around the same time as the Song mission; the Song offer encouraged Chinggis Khan to refuse the Jurchens' peace terms. As their prospects grew bleaker, new rulers came to both the Jin and Xia thrones at the end of 1223. By the time Chinggis Khan had reached Mongolia late in 1224, the two formerly hostile neighbors had begun negotiating a new treaty of friendship. At the same time, however, Tangut envoys continued to travel north to the Mongol khan's *ordo* as well, judging from scraps of official letters, one dating to the second month of 1225, dug up in the desert sands along the former Xia frontier in the early twentieth century. Less than a year later, the khan had set out once more to subdue a rebellious subject. By that time, Tangut refusal to submit a royal hostage to the Mongol court, as was customary (the sons of submitted rulers served in Chinggis's imperial guard), numbered among their crimes of defiance.

Final Movements

Accounts of the Mongol warrior's last campaign are inevitably bound up with the legends and tales about his death and secretive burial in Mongolia. To the day of this writing his burial site remains a mystery, one so alluring as to attract millions of dollars in Japanese and American investment in recent attempts to locate and unearth the tomb; even if found it is unlikely to contain any treasure of significance. So far the conqueror remains undisturbed in his final resting place under Burkhan Khaldun, the Mongols' sacred peak in the Khentii Range.

In the *Secret History*'s account of Chinggis Khan's final movements, as the Mongol chief advanced south toward the Xia border in the winter of 1225–1226, he stopped to hunt wild asses and was thrown from his horse, sustaining a serious injury. Forced to pitch camp and await the khan's recovery, the Mongols sent envoys to the Tangut ruler, warning him of the consequences of their earlier actions. Once again the bold Asha Gambu spoke up and haughtily dared the Mongols to come seek Tangut riches in their mountain encampments. If the ailing khan had wavered, these words stiffened his resolve; if the Mongols needed justification to lay waste the Tangut realms, this taunt supplied it for posterity: "Because the Tangut people gave their word but did not keep it, Chinggis-khan for the second time took the field against them." Perhaps the Mongols would indeed have withdrawn had the Tanguts demonstrated a convincingly penitent attitude. At this point, however, the Tanguts were counting on their recently concluded alliance with Jin, miscalculating both Jurchen weakness and Mongol strength.

In the second month of 1226, Mongol armies began to pick off Tangut fortifications in the west, circling around back toward the cities on the Yellow River, where in the tenth month they laid siege to Lingzhou, just south of the capital. Along the way, local Tangut defenders surrendered, or resisted and were slaughtered. Despite the resistance offered by the garrison in the western city of

Ganzhou, Chahan, a longtime trusted officer in the Mongol army and a Ganzhou native and son of the Tangut defense commander, managed to secure a pardon for the city's population. As Mongol troops approached the capital area, the new Tangut ruler reportedly died of fright, and his unfortunate successor continued in vain to dispatch troops against the invaders. After the collapse of Lingzhou in December 1226, witnessed by the khan's aide, Yelü Chucai, Chinggis left an army to surround the capital and moved south, crossing the Yellow River again, to conquer the territories of present-day southern Gansu. In the late spring of 1227, he halted at the Liupan Mountains in southeastern Ningxia to "escape the heat." It took Mongol troops six months to overcome the Tangut capital's defenses, but its king finally surrendered in the sixth month of 1227. According to the terms of surrender, the Tangut ruler presented himself with a large treasure to the khan. It is likely that Chinggis had already died at his camp, sometime in August.

The Mysteries of Death

Not surprisingly, the *Secret History* keeps Chinggis alive until after his adversary had made obeisance outside the khan's tent and then been led off to his doom. Mongol troops sacked the Tangut capital, as customary, slaughtered many of its inhabitants, and ravaged the Tangut imperial tombs, in revenge for Chinggis's death or perhaps, as Igor de Rachwiltz speculates, to transform them into guardian spirits accompanying the khan in his afterlife. The reputation of the Xia rulers as powerful Buddhist kings suggested special handling. Killing such a vessel of religious potency, whom the *Secret History* refers to by what were evidently native epithets of Burkhan khan (Buddha king) or Ilukhu Burkhan (victorious Buddha), required proper ritual preparation. Hence, Chinggis Khan (or his surrogates) gave the surrendered Tangut king the nickname Shidurghu, "Upright," in order to turn the former enemy into a protective spirit (if it was not a derisive commentary on the Tangut ruler's lack of loyalty, a death sentence rite, in short).

In other thirteenth-century sources Chinggis died of an illness that brought on high fever. It may be that the Mongols did not know the precise cause of his death, and that the circumstances surrounding his expiration, the surrender of the Xia Buddha-king, and the bloodbath visited upon the Tanguts were so unsavory as to invite obfuscation. This may explain why seventeenth-century Mongolian chronicles and later folklore weave tales of murder at the hands of the Tangut queen. In these stories, after destroying the Tangut country, Chinggis took the beautiful Tangut queen to bed as his prize. But she hid a sharp object within herself and thus inflicted a mortal wound on the khan, presumably to avenge her people, then cast herself into the Yellow River, becoming a local river deity.

Despite the charge of perfidy that cost the Tanguts their kingdom and the khan's life, the Mongols treated surrendered Tanguts well and recruited them to positions of responsibility in their conquest establishment. Like other central Asians and unlike the Jurchens, Khitans, and Chinese, during the Yuan dynasty Tanguts held the privileged legal status of the *semu* (assorted kinds), foreign collaborators second in status only to the Mongols themselves. The Buddhist traditions of the Xia court survived, through the efforts of Tangut and Tibetan intermediaries, into the Yuan and blossomed at Khubilai's court later in the thirteenth century.

Because of the deliberate secrecy surrounding the demise of the world conqueror and the vagueness of the historical records, legends have sprung up from that day forward with fantastic details of his death and burial: That everyone encountered in the path of the funeral cortege from north China to northeast Mongolia was killed to ensure secrecy; that the summer heat and the lack of knowledge about embalming forced the Mongols to bury the khan in the Ordos (the loop within the Yellow River, in today's Inner Mongolian Autonomous Region of China) or at least to cremate him; that the funeral procession got bogged down in the Ordos and so the khan found his resting place there; that only his ashes reached Burkhan Khaldun; and so on. Scholars doubt that anything of material value is buried in the khan's grave, wherever it might lie.

Chinggis's Successors

A two-year interregnum followed Chinggis Khan's death, during which his youngest son Tolui acted as regent for the empire until the 1229 *khuriltai* on the Kherlen River, which formally installed the third son, Ögedei, as the new great khan (*khaghan*, a title which Chinggis had not officially adopted). Chinggis had earlier selected his third son to succeed him, or rather, he approved Chaghadai's suggestion that Ögedei should succeed their father rather than the "Merkit bastard" Jochi. In any case, Jochi had already died. Unlike his older brothers and father, Ögedei had a congenial, liberal, and open personality, and preferred drinking to campaigning. Rashid al-Din and other chroniclers have immortalized his extravagant generosity in numerous anecdotes.

Nevertheless, Ögedei extended and institutionalized his father's achievements, employing the extraordinary talents of many able Mongol generals. During his twelve-year reign, north China came under Mongol control with the demise of the Jin dynasty in 1234; the new khaghan laid the first plans for the conquest of Song China in the south; a Mongol expeditionary army established contact with Tibet that brought the Tibetans into a special relationship with the empire; a new imperial capital began to rise in central Mongolia at Kharakhorum in 1235; and the Qipchaq steppe and Russian principalities had fallen to Mongol armies by 1240. Mongol troops advanced into eastern Europe, halting only when news of the great khan's death in 1241 reached their commanders, who quickly prepared to return to Mongolia for the all-important *khuriltai*, which would elect the next khan. Europeans have been grateful ever since for the serendipitous timing of Ögedei's passing. The great khan's main wife, Töregene, became regent, initiating a prolonged period of political instability and factional fighting that ended the first phase of the Mongols' mission as "world conquerors."

Assessing the Mongol Khan

Chinggis Khan emerges from the thirteenth- and fourteenth-century sources as a compelling personality, a formidable strategist, an astute judge of character, and a severe man of great self-discipline. An "accursed infidel" in early Muslim chronicles of the time, in others he becomes an unparalleled hero whose deeds paved the way for an expansion of the realm of Islam.

Rashid al-Din's evaluation of Chinggis Khan's career bespeaks a general understanding among the Il-khanid allies of Great Khan Khubilai (1260–1294):

> Despite his setbacks and the multiplicity of difficulties, he was magnificently brave and courageous as well as extremely intelligent, skilled, farsighted, and cultured. His name and reputation for generosity and beneficence spread in all directions, affection for him appeared in all natures, and nations inclined to him so that he grew strong and mighty and rendered his friends victorious and prosperous and his enemies vanquished and despised.

"Cultured" is not an association readily made with the Mongol conqueror, but Juvaini paints Chinggis as lawgiver, creator of writing and record-keeping for the Mongols, reformer of "reprehensible customs," and tolerant and reasonable overlord who "honoured and respected the learned and pious of every sect" and dispensed with empty formalism and pretentious ritual. Juvaini also compares Chinggis to an earlier conqueror, Alexander, who "had he lived in the age of Chingiz-Khan, would have been his pupil in craft and cunning. . . ." Mongol patronage of Muslim courts and courtiers, and the eventual conversion of many Mongols to Islam, goes far to explain the largely positive image that the Mongol conqueror enjoys in later Muslim writings of the era.

The Mongol warrior's physical presence impressed followers and observers as unusual. Zhao Hong, a Song Chinese envoy to north China under Mongol occupation in ca. 1221, recorded a description undoubtedly provided by his Mongol hosts (Chinggis being in central Asia at the time). After noting that Tatars, as the Mongol conquerors at first referred to themselves, tended to be short and ugly, Zhao Hong

Figure 9.1 Portrayal of Chinggis Khan in a ger (tent) camp wall hanging (looking less Chinese) © Ruth Dunnell/Ruth W. Dunnell.

remarks that the "Tatar lord Temüjin differs in that he is of noble bearing with a broad forehead and long whiskers and cuts a heroic and robust figure." Other writers have commented on his piercing eyes. Allegedly Chinggis had no gray hair and kept his health up to the year of his death, at around age 66. In other words, we have here the portrait of an idealized nomadic khan, whose cruelties were divinely ordained and whose genius lay in the prudent disposal of people and resources toward the fulfillment of laudable goals: requiting wrongs and establishing an orderly, well-provisioned society.

Certainly the *Secret History* portrays the khan as taking life's lessons to heart and keeping a mind open to criticism and counsel from many kinds of people, including the women close to him. An ambitious man, Chinggis disciplined his passions, but once decided upon a course of action he pursued it implacably to its conclusion. Thus he acquired the reputation of a great ruler, more politician and tactician than fighter; a man who attracted equally ambitious and talented youths to his cause and cemented their loyalties through the clear, generous and, for those times, fair terms of treatment he accorded his followers.

As Chinggis Khan moved out of the Mongolian plateau, his successes and a reputation for rewarding loyalty and practical skills ensured that the Mongol cause would not suffer from lack of talent and manpower. If nomads cherished adaptability and generosity above all, demanding that their leaders share with them the deprivations as well as the glories of the hunt, then it is not surprising that we find in our sources a khan who displayed those qualities in abundance. It was expected, too, that he guard his prerogatives as khan, and followers who infringed upon their master's rights or violated his laws paid the penalty.

In punishing enemies and dealing with lawbreakers, Chinggis Khan exercised deadly ruthlessness, deemed in many sources as a sign of his wisdom and divine justification. Perhaps uniquely motivated by the desire to wreak vengeance on all those who had crossed his path as a youth growing up, Chinggis turned a quest for power into a vision of a new social and moral order for the Mongol tribes that gradually came to encompass the world touched by the hoofs of his armies' horses. Later, anyone who defied his call to order and submission justified their own liquidation, by the most efficient means available: Deliberate terror (psychological warfare) followed by wholesale slaughter.

Yet there is no evidence to support a Mongol sanction for the more sensational and grisly tales of atrocity that circulated in those years and down to the present. Unlike some of his enemies, Chinggis, a man of considerable emotional restraint, appeared neither to have derived particular pleasure from torturing or inflicting sadistic deaths on people, nor to have resorted to such tactics as a matter of revenge or military procedure. Greed, or rather gain, might provoke Mongol troops to depart from standard operating procedure, as in the tale related by Juvaini about the punishment of one defiant town in central Asia:

> When the Mongols finished the slaughter they caught sight of a woman who said to them: 'Spare my life and I will give you a great pearl which I have.' But when they sought the pearl she said: 'I have swallowed it.' Whereupon they ripped open her belly and found several pearls. Upon this account Chingiz-Khan commanded that they should rip open the bellies of all the slain.

Here Mongol troops dealt with a defiant resister and then reported the treasure to their khan, as required. Recovering valuable resources from corpses (apart from the unwise woman who could not even keep her own bargain!) made economic sense, and did not spring from a need to gratify uncontrollable lust for killing.

Appreciating the attraction of unaccustomed wealth and comfort, the khan was also inspired by the desire to prevent the dissolution of nomadic hardiness in future generations, at the same time that he found satisfaction in sharing the luxuries reaped by his successes. In one anecdote preserved by Rashid al-Din, Chinggis commented wryly, "[a]fter us, our offspring will wear gold-brocaded robes and eat sweet and fatty tidbits. They will ride beautiful horses and embrace lovely ladies. They will not say, 'These things were assembled by our fathers and elders.' On that day of greatness they will forget us." The khan intended his *yasakh*, or moral commandments, to protect them: "Henceforth, for however many years. . . . that my offspring will come into existence and rule as khans, my progeny, no matter how grand they may become, will safeguard themselves with the. . . . *yosun* [norms] and *yasaq* and will not replace it. They will enjoy favor from heaven, and they will always have pleasure and enjoyment."

At the center of the idealized Mongol khan's moral vision was absolute loyalty to friends and family, to one's ruler, and to the group upon whom one depended. Loyalty and betrayal indeed frame the case that the *Secret History* and other sources produced at Mongol courts make for their founding father. It is clear that the khan indulged in as much treachery as he condemned in others, but luck and treachery alone cannot explain his survival and accomplishments. Chinggis depended on many people who guarded and cared for him, fought for him, fed and provisioned his people, opened up for them new channels of trade and communication with the outside world, wrote down the Mongols' laws and kept the records, and raised and educated their children. Always, until Khubilai came to power in China, the nomadic core of this expanding universe, the Golden Lineage and their ablest commanders (the *noyan*), remained the focus of concern and loyalty for Chinggis and his successors. The intense esprit de corps generated among the inner circle during the lifetimes of Chinggis and Ögedei, his first successor, carried the Mongols onto the stage of world history as peerless conquerors.

With the succession of Tolui's sons, Möngke in 1251 and then Khubilai in 1260, that esprit de corps dissolved, and the empire as a collective enterprise came slowly undone. Khubilai made a brilliant career in China, laying no less than the foundations of the modern Chinese nation, but the Mongol Empire as such ceased to exist, spinning off regional empires in competition with one another. Nevertheless, the career of Chinggis, as enshrined and embellished in legends and historical chronicles, provided the touchstone of moral authority and political legitimation, a kind of constitution, for would-be khans in the transformed landscape of Eurasia. In this respect, the Mongols departed from their steppe predecessors, for the geohistorical stage on which their play unfolded presented far greater opportunities for imprinting the future, and not just for Mongolia, where Chinggis has been revived as the national symbol and father figure of the post–cold war Mongolian state. The far-reaching consequences of that imprint are explored in more detail in Chapter 10.

Legacies: The Mongol Empire, Eurasian History, and Modern Mongolia

The rise and progress of the Ottomans, the present sovereigns of Constantinople, are connected with the most important scenes of modern history; but they are founded on a previous knowledge of the great eruption of the Moguls and Tartars. . . .

EDWARD GIBBON, THE DECLINE AND FALL OF THE ROMAN EMPIRE

Writing about Chinggis Khan and the impact of his conquests has occupied many scribes over the centuries. Among the descendants of people who suffered the brunt of the Mongols' brutal onslaught in the early thirteenth century, the verdict on the Mongols varies according to prevailing political or religious needs. This is especially true for twentieth-century nationalist histories. Chinese revolutionaries eventually embraced them because, among other things, the Mongols greatly expanded China's borders and needed to be enlisted in the struggle against Japanese imperialism. In the stories that Muslims from the thirteenth century to the seventeenth century wrote about him, Chinggis first became a monotheistic tool of God, then a source of political legitimation for many rulers. But, Michal Biran argues, with the emergence of modern nation states from the nineteenth century on, the grounds upon which earlier generations had praised the conqueror crumbled. Muslim writers, according to their local circumstances (and influenced by European stereotypes), began rejecting him as a foreign infidel and barbaric destroyer, the archetypal Oriental despot. The 2003 American invasion of Iraq elicited unflattering Arab comparisons with the thirteenth-century Mongol siege of Baghdad.

Mongol armies indeed massacred large numbers of people and enslaved many others, destroyed towns and cities as well as thousands of acres of arable land, and may have inadvertently facilitated the spread of the bacillus that causes bubonic plague. From China to Europe, millions of people (including nomads) died of plague in the fourteenth century. Though the plague ended a great era of Eurasian travel and exchange, the spread of plague bacillus was just one product of the intercivilizational exchanges fostered by the Mongols. Careful scholarship over the last fifty years shows that the Mongols bequeathed a rich and many-faceted legacy comparable to the subsequent impact of expanding Europe on the Old World (or what used to be called the third world). Throughout the thirteenth and fourteenth centuries, the Mongols' relationship to the sedentary civilizations with which they interacted changed continuously, as befitted a highly adaptable people. In its conquests, governing policies, and disintegration, the Mongol Empire transformed the identities of many peoples (including the Mongols themselves), destroyed some outright, and created new ethnic groups and polities in their wake.

Above all, the Mongols created new cultural syntheses wherever they ruled, combining their own steppe practices and military-political structures with the economic, administrative, and cultural elements of the people whom they recruited and among whom they settled, be they Muslim Turkic nomads, Persian clerics, or Chinese bureaucrats. A distinctive Mongol imperial culture emerged and was widely shared across the empire even after its breakup into rival khanates (see Map 6.1). Core Mongol beliefs, policies, and imperial practices defined a "Chinggisid dispensation," which framed the political landscape of large parts of Eurasia for centuries afterward.

Elements of Mongol Imperial Culture

Five elements in the Chinggisid legacy stand out from the narrative presented in the previous chapters: (1) the notion of universal sovereignty justifying righteous conquest; (2) the empire as joint property of the royal clan (in both the political and economic realms); (3) Chinggisid legitimacy; (4) court protocols (hunting and drinking); and (5) patronage of trade through merchant partnerships (*ortogh*) and employment of nonnative specialists (such as merchants) to administer conquered territories. These elements, many derived from earlier steppe practices and experiences, put a distinctive Mongol brand on the territories under their sway that outlasted the brutally efficient early Mongolian war machine.

1. As narrated in the earlier chapters, the man who became Chinggis Khan in 1206 was driven by the ambition to avenge wrongs to himself, his clan, and his tribe. In surviving setbacks while pursuing his ambition, he became convinced that Tengri, Heaven, favored him above all others and had great designs for him. It took several decades for Tengri's design to reveal its full extent. A turning point came with the 1218 murder of Chinggis Khan's envoys and trade delegation at Otrar.

Khwarazm-shah Muhammad's reckless reply to the Mongol khan's overtures set the Mongol conquest machine in operation, and it did not come to rest until late in the century. No longer were the Mongols content to punish the Jin court in north China and exact tribute from it. Because refusal to submit to the Mongols was tantamount to defiance of Heaven, nothing less than the annihilation of the perfidious Jin emperor and his minions, and the absorption of the population into the Mongol state, sufficed.

Bolstered with new ideas absorbed through sedentary advisors, Chinggis Khan's successors developed to its fullest the ideology of world dominion, clearly expressed in their letters to distant rulers demanding submission. Great Khan Güyüg's letter in 1246 to Pope Innocent IV models the approach, opening with the words, "We, by the power of Eternal Heaven," and concluding, "If you do not observe God's command, and if you ignore my command, I shall know you as my enemy. Likewise I shall make you understand." Mongol armies did not burst forth unbridled to plunder and maim at will. Because their numbers were small they practiced a ruthless economy of war, deploying the discipline of the hunt, deliberate terror, exaggeration, deceit, and other devices to attain victory. Campaigns of conquest followed from the logic of divinely sanctioned vengeance and world sovereignty; battles typically were preceded by the visit of a Mongol envoy, demanding surrender and warning of the consequences of resistance. For most of the thirteenth century, the Mongols became instruments of God; you were either with them or you were against them, at least in theory.

2 & 3. The second and third elements, the empire as joint property of the royal clan and Chinggisid legitimacy, are closely linked. The Mongols understood the empire as property belonging to the Chinggisid ruling clan, not to an individual khan. By nomadic custom all members of the Golden Lineage, Chinggis Khan's brothers, principal sons, their wives, and their descendants, were expected to share in the rewards of their collaborative efforts. They and their wives received shares (appanages or *qubi*) in the conquered territories and had the right to designate agents to collect revenue from those shares, that is, from the people inhabiting the land designated in their deeded share. Thus Chinggisid princes in Mongolia had agents collecting revenues from Golden Horde territories, Qipchaq princes posted representatives to oversee appanages in China, and so on. Whatever local administrative and fiscal chaos this might and did engender, it remained a fiercely defended right of Chinggisids, and became a bone of contention among them when more centralizing great khans came to power, such as Möngke (1251–1259) and Khubilai (1260–1294). Indeed, it wove a net of relationships across the vast expanse of Eurasia that offset the fissiparous tendencies of the empire and enabled cultural exchange to occur.

Leadership was also shared in the clan. The Mongols did not practice primogeniture (the eldest son inheriting the father's position or property), and each succession opened up new rounds of struggle among eligible candidates for the khan-ship, which by custom included all brothers, sons, and nephews of a khan. The only succession to escape open contention brought Chinggis's third son Ögedei to power in 1229; only Chinggis himself had the authority to confirm his successor and he did so in part by keeping a tight rein on his own brothers. Thus economic disorder at the local level had its counterpart in political instability and factional intrigue at court that often paralyzed the great khan's central government. Mongol political culture remained highly personalized and patrimonial, both a strength and a weakness.

Chinggisid legitimacy refers to the solidly established tradition bequeathed by the Mongol Empire to Eurasia that only bona fide descendants of the Golden Lineage could become a khan. Chinggisid rulers of the various khanates continued to acquire their primary wives only from other high-ranking Mongol clans. Other powerful Turko-Mongol leaders, such as the fourteenth-century conqueror Tamerlane (Timur the Lame), had to content themselves with the lesser title of emir or commander, and rule through puppet khans. Although non-Chinggisid Mongol dynasties arose later on in central and southwest Asia, India, and the Middle East, the special position, if not the power, of Chinggis Khan's descendants (the Borjigins) persisted in Mongolia.

A remarkable result of the charisma of Chinggisid legitimacy came to light in 2003, when geneticists reported that about 8 percent of males from the Pacific Ocean to the Caspian Sea (0.5 percent of the world total) carry a gene apparently originating in Mongolia within the past thousand years. The findings confirm that Chinggis's descendants, who practiced polygamy (multiple simultaneous legal wives) as well as took concubines, succeeded through more than one method in offsetting their small numbers in the social realm to perpetuate their lineages and rule over large parts of Asia. Killing off the population during conquest would not alone guarantee this genetic outcome.

4. Imperial Mongol court culture was both highly aristocratic and often informal. Mongol nobles, both men and women, became enthusiastic patrons of the refined arts of Persian painting and poetry, various religious orders, and the Chinese theater; they routinely participated in drinking parties that went on for days. A prominent feature of court life, celebratory feasts could require daily changes of costly color-coordinated robes, distributed to the numerous guests as a mark of imperial favor, and the consumption of vast quantities of diverse alcoholic beverages. Mongol fondness for spirituous liquor stimulated their production, and consequently techniques for distilling alcohol as well as names for such drinks, spread from East to West.

Woven from gold and silk threads, the brocade cloth used to make court robes, as well as princely tents and palanquins, employed thousands of artisans transported from central Asia and China to work in Mongol workshops. These brocades became famous throughout Europe and Asia as "Tartar cloth." Marco Polo was only one of many observers who depicted in word or image the extravagant garments arrayed at court feasts. On the occasion of a birthday party, Great Khan Khubilai appeared in a robe of "beaten gold," attended by twelve thousand courtiers in similar robes of silk and gold, "though not so costly"; yet adds the sharp-eyed Venetian, "I will aver that there are some of these suits decked with so many pearls and precious stones that a single suit shall be worth full 10,000 golden bezants [medieval coin]." If we recall Börte's sable coat that Temüjin presented to Ong-khan and the quilt embroidered with pearls taken by Temüjin in the 1196 Tatar campaign, we can better appreciate the significant role played by the presentation of luxurious raiment in framing the empire: The search for wealth and power to produce and then distribute such robes and other fine gifts constituted the central axis along which Mongol power was generated and displayed itself.

Entertainments (for example singing, wrestling, and acrobatics), hunting parties, and lavish bestowal of gifts accompanied festive court gatherings. The overt rowdiness of such occasions masks their strategic political and ritual functions: to manifest the majesty, generosity, and wealth of the khan; to establish hierarchies of subordination while generating a spirit of shared identity; to recognize and confirm alliances through gift-giving and communal hunts; and to propitiate protective spirits and make offerings to Tengri. Being invited to hunt with the khan was a sign of royal favor and an occasion for politicking. For commanders and ordinary soldiers, hunts also served as training exercises for war during the winter months.

5. The Mongol policy of promoting and patronizing long-distance trade and merchants continued a steppe nomadic tradition of active participation in Eurasian trade, both overland and by sea. As the Introduction pointed out, nomads had often served to protect central Asian merchants by patrolling the caravan routes. Loving their luxuries like the rest of us, steppe nomads acquired tea, grain, textiles, and metal implements through trade. As a matter of policy Mongol khans and aristocrats gave gold or gems from their treasuries to merchants to invest for them and employed capable merchants as tax collectors, finance ministers, and administrators of one sort or another. Merchant agents to Mongol aristocrats, called *ortogh* (Turk, "partners"), were Muslims or Uighurs (who might be Christian, Buddhist, or Muslim) from central Asia, and received special authorization, in the form of gold, silver, or bronze tablets (*paiza*, from Chinese), that gave them tax exemptions and access to all the amenities of the Mongols' well-organized and frequently abused network of post roads and relay stations. Many Mongol aristocrats became indebted to their merchant partners in order to keep their palace-tents supplied with the costliest foods, garments, beverages, and other items needed to maintain the lifestyle befitting their status.

Sedentary subjects of the Mongols in Persia and China hated the merchants for their usurious moneylending and incessant requisitioning of goods and taxes. But merchants were not the only specialists employed by the Mongols to help them conquer and administer their empire. Persian and Chinese engineers taught them siege craft, enabling them to take heavily fortified walled cities and expand their empire in ways that earlier steppe warriors could not. Mobilizing foreign expertise (initially Chinese) allowed the Mongols to create an artillery unit for use in Iran, encouraging the spread of gunpowder to Europe. Muslim cartographers, astronomers, and mathematicians introduced Persian sciences to China through the Yuan court's activities; doctors of every stripe served the Mongol elite and disseminated knowledge of Chinese, Persian, Arabic, and Eastern Christian medical practices around Eurasia. Mongol imperial priorities drove their quest for goods, services, and knowledge, all of which stimulated the circulation of things throughout the empire. Political and administrative expediency made routine the employment of skilled, multicultural foreigners who were loyal to their overlords in areas such as Persia and Yuan China, where resistance by hostile native elites simmered just below the surface.

The Mongol love of luxuries also fed a new Chinese fashion in gemstones, imported by Muslim traders from west Asia, along with Arab books about gems and minerals. Chinese writers recorded this new knowledge, and called the stones *Huihui shitou*, "Muslim rocks," or *baohuo*, "precious goods." Gemstones became a significant Yuan import, by sea and overland trade routes. Despite continued criticism from Confucian officials, the subsequent Ming dynasty went even further in the pursuit of "precious stones." The early fifteenth-century voyages of Zheng He sailed out in fleets called *baochuan*, "precious boats," in pursuit of gems, among other items. Ming "gem fever" fostered expanded trade with north Burma, exchanging Chinese silver (from Yunnan mines, mainly) for Burmese jewels.

These five elements in the Mongol imperial tradition affected different regions of Mongol-dominated Asia to varying degrees, and all of them to some degree, and often accelerated other historical trends. As already noted, by the late thirteenth century the Mongol conquests had advanced the process of the Turkicization and Islamization of Eurasia, making it more accurate to use the term *Turko-Mongol empires* throughout this period. Many Mongols who stayed in east Asia ended up as Tibetan Buddhists; those who went west became Islamized and Turkicized along with much of the central and west Asian population. Some peoples swept up in the conquests, such as the Buddhist Tanguts whose state was destroyed in 1227, ended up becoming Muslims when the Mongol overlord of their homeland in Gansu converted to Islam.

Though few Yuan Mongols, apart from that prince, became Muslim, a significant population of Muslims of central Asian origin participated in the conquests of north and south China, and settled there as members of the ruling establishment, forming the basis of China's contemporary Hui (Chinese Muslim) ethnic minority. In the southeast Chinese coastal cities, they displaced the leaders of earlier Muslim Arab trading communities. Most Mongol aristocrats in China under the Yuan dynasty subscribed to Tibetan Buddhism, Nestorian Christianity, Confucianism, or some combination of these mixed with native Tengri worship and shamanic practices.

The Yuan emperors incorporated Tibet loosely into their empire, and first tried to rule the region through one of the newer contending lineages of revived Tibetan Buddhism. Local disorder forced them to pull Tibet under their administrative umbrella. At the same time Khubilai patronized the powerful Tibetan Sakya sect and appointed its clerics to serve as "imperial preceptors," the royal family's religious teachers and ritual guides, though the activities of the privileged Buddhist monks (Tibetan and others) in China extended far beyond the court. Although most of the Mongol nobility abandoned Buddhism after fleeing China in the mid-fourteenth century, reconverting again en masse in the late sixteenth century, the history of the relationship between Tibetan lamas and Mongol emperors serves to buttress contemporary claims by the Chinese government over the territory of Tibet.

The Turko-Mongol dynasties in both Iran and southern Russia (Golden Horde) eventually converted to Islam and became Turkic speaking in the fourteenth century. Mongolian remained mainly a diplomatic and chancery language (and not the only one). In all the khanates, tracing one's descent from the Chinggisids and their close companions (*nököd*) constituted an assertion of political privilege as much as a statement of ethnic identity.

Mongol Imperial Culture in East Asia and Persia

Because China and Persia contained the two richest regions of the Mongol Empire with long-established sedentary agrarian bureaucracies, in the late thirteenth century they became closely allied in the struggle of Khubilai Khan (r. 1260–1294) and his branch of Chinggisids against the other branches, who objected to Khubilai's strategy of occupying these territories permanently and not sharing their wealth with the other Chinggisid princes. The significance of this development to Chinggis Khan's legacy and the generation of the historical sources upon which any history of the Mongol Empire depends justifies a description of its contours here.

In 1253, Great Khan Möngke (r. 1251–1259) sent his younger brother Hülegü (d. 1265) to establish order in Iraq and Iran, at the request of local Muslim authorities who complained about both the oppressive exactions of the local Mongol governor and Ismaili sectarian violence. The Great Khan intended to eliminate the 'Abbasid Caliph of Bagdad, the Sunni ruler of Iraq, who had for several decades refused to acknowledge Mongol claims. Hülegü first put an end to the Ismailis, an extremist and secretive Shi'ite sect headquartered in the mountains of northern Persia (eastern Iran) and popularly known as the *Order of Assassins*, after their techniques of converting and dispatching enemies. They had terrorized the region for over a century, but the Mongol cleansing sent them underground for many years.

Hülegü went on to conquer Baghdad in 1258, and stayed to found the Il-khanate, a Mongol dynasty formally subordinate to the great khan in China, but independent for all practical purposes. By the dawn of the fourteenth century, the Il-khanids had embraced Islam, the religion of their subjects. Extensive exchanges of goods, people, technologies, and ideas took place between China and Persia. From early on the Mongols had applied similar governing techniques in both areas, as demonstrated in the careers of Mahmud Yalavic, who held important official positions in both central Asia and north China, and Yelü Chucai, who served Mongol governors in north China; both counseled the Mongols on how to rule sedentary peoples . Close ties between the two courts often pitted the steppe khanates of central Asia and the Qipchaq khanate, led by the progeny of Chinggis's other sons, against the Yuan rulers and Persian Il-khans, both descended from Tolui, the youngest son. Hostility between the Il-khans and the Qipchaq rulers arising from competition over adjoining territories in the

Caucasus (still a contested region), such as Azerbaijan, also became a permanent feature of regional relationships.

The mix of Islamic, Mongol, Persian, and Chinese elements in the Il-khanid and Yuan dynasties produced a uniquely cosmopolitan and vibrant cultural efflorescence, in part a result of the close political and economic relationship between the two courts. In the Qipchaq steppe, a similar dynamic syncretism produced the medieval Russian state. Cultural contact and exchange between China and Persia predated the Mongol Empire, but Yuan developments stimulated direct and close ties between China and Persia/Iran for over half a century.

Because it became the seat of the great khans, China underwent significant changes in the thirteenth and fourteenth centuries. China's borders expanded and its population became more diverse. Yunnan in southwest China, like Tibet formerly outside the Chinese realm, was absorbed into the Yuan Empire by a Muslim general during the conquest of south China; thus a sizable Muslim (Hui) population inhabits Yunnan to the present day.

The Mongols ruled China largely through Muslims and central Asians, and favored Han or northern Chinese (the Yuan category of "Han" included former Jin subjects—Khitans, Jurchens, and Chinese—and Koreans) over southerners. Many Confucian elites found themselves in retirement or trying out new occupations. This overturning of the former social order had numerous effects, some quite energizing for Chinese culture, others unexpected or paradoxical. Rich southerners did not, however, face confiscation of their estates; the Mongols never tried to reform the uneven distribution of wealth (land) in south China.

Reduced to a special status category with a low glass ceiling, the former southern Song elites became clerks, teachers, doctors, or fortune-tellers, unless they had the family resources to retire to a life of painting, poetry, and scholarship. In Yuan society, it became more acceptable to engage in previously stigmatized occupations such as writing for the theater. Likewise, the status of people with "practical" occupations rose: Merchants, artisans, doctors, astronomers, legal and administrative experts, and engineers found favor and employment in the new Yuan order.

Nevertheless, in the early fourteenth century concerted efforts by Confucian officials (Chinese and those of foreign origin) at the Yuan court led to the revival of the Chinese civil service examination system in 1315. The examinations did not become an important avenue of recruitment to Yuan office; because of an equal quota allotted across all categories of people taking them, they tended to boost the fortunes of literary-minded Mongol and Semu (foreign collaborators) candidates, who were a tiny percent of the total population, more than that of the Chinese. Their revival, though, was one index of Mongol elite involvement in Chinese culture, and the political ramifications of that involvement were controversial.

Mongol attempts in the reign of Khubilai (1260–1294) to impose on the Yuan population at large their own marriage custom of levirate, loathsome to Confucians, led to a series of compromise measures crafted by officials (both Chinese and central Asian) in the Ministry of Rites. By these rulings, for the first time in Chinese history widows lost the right to return to their natal homes and enter into new marriages with their dowry. The measures boosted efforts, and were likely motivated by the desire, to consolidate the resources and authority of clan and lineage elders at the expense of juniors such as sons and wives; they also aimed to ensure that households with military responsibilities had the means to meet them, which was the original Mongol concern. This legal development supported a new cultural commitment to the old ideal of widow chastity, that is, rewarding young widows who did not remarry or even killed themselves to protect their "virtue" (i.e., loyalty to the lineage) that became a hallmark of late imperial Chinese society. Moreover, it contributed to the rise of powerful corporate lineages, another distinctive feature of the late imperial Chinese landscape.

Such a change in Chinese legal practice with far-reaching social implications might never have occurred under a native dynasty, but the crisis created by foreign occupation for Chinese elites, who had been thrown out of work and had their identity and status severely compromised, fostered conditions that allowed such shifts to occur. In particular for southern members of the traditional Confucian-trained ruling elite, the Mongol occupation sharpened and narrowed their notions of what it meant to be "Chinese"; living under Mongol rule fostered a xenophobic patriotism in some Chinese, at the very time when more different kinds of people were becoming "Chinese."

In fact, the Mongols never reached agreement on how to rule China. Mongol political culture was at core consultative; no matter how powerful a khan, decisions about the ends toward which he exercised his power were first reached, or publicly affirmed, in an assembly of nobles. Once the conquests were over, the tasks of ruling remained, collecting and distributing revenue from the subject populations being principal among them. In circumventing the traditional Chinese elite, the Yuan government invested considerable authority in local clerks and non-Chinese overseers, which made it increasingly difficult for the center to control outlying provinces.

After Khubilai (d. 1294), political issues at stake in succession struggles at the Yuan court revolved around the tensions between loyalty to Chinggis's vision of empire, as embodied in the five elements discussed earlier, and effectiveness in ruling China. With no consensus on occupying China (a consensus that the Manchus later achieved), the Mongols could not find a balance between exacting wealth and maintaining order: the essential tasks of all Chinese regimes (and all modern states, one might argue). Their government collapsed in the mid-fourteenth century under many challenges, both natural and man-made.

Yet because the Mongols ruled in the guise of Chinese emperors, permanently enlarged the territory of China, and facilitated the influx of many ethnic groups who became part of the fabric of Chinese society in subsequent centuries, nationalist Chinese historians in the modern era have been willing to acknowledge their positive contributions to Chinese history. The Mongol and Manchu legacies make it easier for the Chinese to accept an identity (and propaganda about it) as a multinational state with legitimate rights to rule Tibetans, Mongols, and other peoples within its present borders.

Mongol Imperial Culture in Russia

To early Russian chroniclers, who were Orthodox churchmen, and to many later Russian historians, on the other hand, the Tartars (Turko-Mongols) and Qipchaq khanate (dubbed the Golden Horde) stood for barbarism and the forces that severed Russia from the stream of civilized history playing out in Europe, perpetuating Russia's cultural and political backwardness up to the present. According to a report in *The Times* of London in January 2004, Russian scientists claim that the Mongol gene for susceptibility to alcoholism is found in roughly half the population of Moscow, which supposedly explains the national Russian weakness.

Some Russian historians, however, have viewed the Mongols as a source of more significant, and not always negative, contributions to Russian history. The Tatars and their allies who settled in the Qipchaq steppe as the Golden Horde and its later offshoots played important roles in the rise and expansion of the Muscovite state from the late fourteenth century on. By the late thirteenth century, Tatar princes and elites had begun to take up service with the contending Russian princes; from the late fourteenth century they constituted an important source of new service nobles for the rising Muscovite state. Nor were Tatar origins considered something to hide, such was the prestige of the Chinggisids. Many sixteenth- and seventeenth-century Russian gentry families traced their ancestry back to Tatar nobles who intermarried with the Russian aristocracy and converted to Orthodox Christianity (though not necessarily in that order). Likewise, the Muscovite state owed much to Tatar administrative and military precedents in its own structures and practices. Those precedents included Islamic as well as modified Chinese and steppe institutions.

It is commonly thought that the Qipchaq khanate survived longer (into the fifteenth century, not counting its successor regimes) than the other Chinggisid regimes because its rulers remained "pure" nomads roaming the steppe, outside and apart from the sedentary peoples whom they taxed and ruled, directly or indirectly. In fact, the Qipchaq khans and their cousins, the Il-khanid and Chaghadaid khans, all continued to nomadize in the steppes around their capital cities. Probably the most sedentarized of the Mongol ruling courts was the Yuan, and even the Yuan emperor–khans lived much of the time in tents erected on the spacious grounds of the imperial palace at Dadu (Beijing) or out on the northern steppes. In the southern Russian steppes, archaeological excavation has revealed a flourishing urban civilization based on the Golden Horde capital at Sarai and other cities where the Tatar nobility lived and created a hybrid culture of sedentary and nomadic elements. Whatever degree of sedentarization occurred among the khanate's ruling clans, they never completely abandoned their nomad roots while becoming appreciative patrons of the pleasures of urban life. The advantage of the Qipchaq khans over their Persian and Chinese counterparts probably lay in the more plentiful pastures surrounding their cities, and the far weaker attractions of the rudimentary economy and culture of the Rus' principalities to their north.

The eventual fragmentation of the Golden Horde, and the Mongol Empire overall, peopled the future territories of the Moscovite, Romanov, and Soviet empires with new polities and ethnic groups in the Volga and Ural regions, Caucasus, and Siberia, not to mention central Asia. One example, the Crimean Tatars, was mentioned in the Introduction. The multiethnic character of the Russian state owes much to this legacy.

Mongol Imperial Legacies to Central and Southwest Asia

The impact of the Mongols on the history of central and southwest Asia—Iran, Iraq, Afghanistan, and the Middle East—presents an even more complex profile. The initial conquests of central Asia under Chinggis Khan thoroughly destroyed the economy of Khurasan, the traditional heart of Persian culture in northeastern Iran, by wrecking its fragile irrigation system and depopulating the region, which never fully recovered. Because they valued horses and trade routes more than agriculture, Mongol military and fiscal policies along with the influx of nomadic cavalry led to a progressive expansion of pasture and a shrinking of farmland.

Yet with the fall of Baghdad to Hülegü's armies in 1258, the center of Muslim civilization completed a long historical shift from the Arab-speaking world to the Turko-Persian one, that is, from the Mediterranean to Persia and central Asia. Through the patronage of Mongol rulers and their successors, a flowering of Islamic culture occurred in the fourteenth and fifteenth centuries: The literary and plastic arts, painting, book illustration, sculpture, and architecture all rose to new heights, enriched by cultural exchanges with China. Moreover, after the Mongols converted to Islam, their continued attachment to native cultural practices such as drinking and hunting tended to encourage patronage of Sufi sects and their charismatic leaders, rather than the orthodox Sunni forms of Islam practiced by the majority of the population under their rule.

In the late fourteenth century much of the Il-khanid territory and the western part of Chaghadai's realm fell under the sway of the ambitious Tamerlane (Timur the Lame), a local Muslim military commander of Mongol–Turkic descent, but not a Chinggisid. Fancying himself another Chinggis Khan (though he did not speak Mongolian), Tamerlane had to be content with the title of emir while ruling through a puppet khan. He pursued his conquests with bloody gusto, leaving behind mountains of skulls and destruction on a scale surpassing even his model. Tamerlane died in 1405, ironically at Otrar, on his way to conquer Ming China, and his empire fell apart. The Timurid courts of his milder descendants, though politically weak, patronized the cultural and artistic renaissance referred to earlier. A Timurid prince, Babur, founded the Mughal Empire in north India in the sixteenth century.

In central Asia, Chinggisid descent and the conqueror's Great *Yasakh*, or code, enjoyed a long afterlife; their invocation and interpretation shaped the politics of the region up through the eighteenth century. What they meant, exactly, varied with the time and place. The *Yasakh*, more metaphor than legal prescription, was juxtaposed with the Muslim law of Shari'a, often to justify some flexible compromise between Islamic practice and nomadic customary law such as drinking koumiss (fermented mare's milk), an essential court ritual. Champions of the *Yasakh* claimed to uphold the traditions of the Turko-Mongol steppe nomads, and the authority of Chinggis Khan, in political and criminal matters, while deferring to Shari'a in matters involving religious, social, and contractual affairs.

Legacies to Mongolia

The Mongol Empire was in origin and character an aristocratic enterprise, tightly focused upon a privileged conquest elite. In its formative years, entrance into the elite remained open to persons of skill and loyalty to Chinggis Khan, but the social structure of the imperial Mongol armies never lost its hierarchical stratification. While Mongol nobles lived in comparative luxury, hard drinking and intriguing tended to cut short their life spans, reduce fertility over time in at least one case (the Il-khans ran out of heirs in the 1330s), and undermine control over their subordinates. The subelite rank-and-file nomad soldiery, especially those stationed in north China and Persia (farther from the steppes), suffered progressive impoverishment and either settled down, having little recourse but to intermarry with the local population and take up farming, or resorted to banditry. Mongolia itself became an economic backwater during the Yuan dynasty (after 1260), although its pastures assured a steady supply of horses and provisions to contenders for the imperial throne in Dadu (Beijing).

Though the Mongol tribal groupings that emerged from the empire never managed to reunify and establish a strong state in Mongolia until the twentieth century, their legacy and their active cooperation made possible the Manchu conquest of China in 1644. Manchu absorption of Mongolia did not, however, bring prosperity or unity to the Mongol masses. Rather, the problem of economic penetration by the Chinese was accelerated (if it did not begin) under Manchu auspices, and remains a critical issue before the Mongols today.

Still, the powerful charisma of Chinggis Khan meant that to generations of Mongols after 1227, he was the "Holy Lord" and the focus of a pervasive religious and political cult. For centuries his descendants enjoyed special status, if no real power, as aristocrats exempt from the usual fate of commoners: taxation, labor service, and corporal punishment. Mongolian society retained the highly stratified and rigid hierarchy that characterized the mature imperial period, and which in later centuries came to include elements of the Buddhist monastic establishment and the Manchu military elites.

In modern times, Mongol debates over the relative merits and faults of their medieval ancestors' deeds inevitably became embroiled in the nationalist politics of the Soviet Union, which supported the 1921 Mongolian Revolution, and China, which did not. Useful for rallying loyalties up through World War II, traditional heroes afterward came under attack by Soviet and Chinese communists, and were again banned in Mongolia. Before the fall of the Mongolian communist state in 1990, however, the name and image of Chinggis Khan began to appear in the posters and slogans of protesters urging the conservative Mongolian regime to follow Gorbachev's policy of *perestroika* (reform) and *glasnost'* (freer expression of public opinion and debate). When the communist

Figure 10.1   Image of Chinggis Khan on a late twentieth-century Mongolian banknote (the tugrit), based on official Yuan (Chinese) portrait © Ruth Dunnell/Ruth W. Dunnell.

government, along with its official disapproval of the feudal and backward war-lord, was dissolved, a new generation of Mongols moved to restore Chinggis to an honored position as the father and symbol of their country, a focus of popu-lar adoration, a vehicle for mass display, and an inspiration for mass marketing. Since the 1990s, his name and image appear almost everywhere and on nearly every-thing imaginable in Mongolia (see Figure 10.1). Early twentieth-century Mongol revolutionaries replaced the mostly defunct Mongolian clan or surnames with Russian-style patronymics (e.g., in Ivan Ivanovich, the latter name is the patronymic and means "son of Ivan"), but when the new democratic government revived surnames in 1998, many Mongol commoners chose Borjigin, the name of Chinggis's clan.

Glossary

Note on romanization: *Mongolian "kh" is rendered "q" in words or names used mainly or exclusively in Turkic and not adopted by the Mongols; for example, although the word* khan *is of Turkic origin (qan), as it entered Mongolian early it is rendered here with "kh." In the pinyin romanization of the Chinese, "x" is pronounced like "sh."* (Mo.) *indicates a Mongolian term;* (Ch.) *a Chinese one. Common alternate spellings are offered in italics at the end of entries.*

Alans: a people of the north Caucasus region, later incorporated into the Mongol Empire under Grand Khan Möngke in the 1250s

Altaic: the linguistic family to which the Mongol, Turkic, and Tungusic (Jurchen, Manchu, etc.) languages belonged, and by extension the cultures of peoples speaking these languages, though not all of them, were steppe nomads (the Jurchens and the Manchus were forest peoples)

altan urukh: "Golden Lineage" or the Chinggisids

Amur River: arises out of northeast Mongolia and forms the present-day border of northeast China (Manchuria) and Russia, flowing into the straits opposite Sakhalin Island

anda: sworn brother, blood brother

beki: an honorable Mongol title often held by sons and daughters of chiefs; often conflated with title or word denoting a shaman; *also begi*

Borjigin: an important chiefly lineage, supplying khans to the Mongols, to which Temüjin belonged

Burkhan Khaldun: sacred mountain of the Mongols in the Khentii Range in eastern Mongolia

Cathay: European name for China, from "Khitai~Khitan" (see Khitan and Liao)

chiliarchy: (Mo.) *mingghan*; unit of one thousand men in inner Asian military organization

darughachi: local governor or administrator left by Mongols in conquered territory

Desht-i Qipchaq: the Qipchaq steppes, north of Lake Balkash and the Caspian, Aral, and Black seas

Hexi: (Ch.) "West of the [Yellow] River," the Tangut territories of Xia in what is now Gansu Province, Ningxia Hui Autonomous Region, and the Inner Mongolia Autonomous Region in China

Jadaran: branch of the Borjigin lineage to which Jamukha belonged

Jalayir: early rivals of the Borjigin Mongol; after being defeated they became a subject tribe or "hereditary slaves" to the Mongols, aiding the rise of Chinggis Khan; most famous was the great general Mukhali

jam: Mongol system of post roads, post stations, and the provisions and services associated with them, to which persons holding certificates or *paizas* had access; *also yam*

jarghuchi: judge (at first also chief scribe) in the Mongol Empire

Jurchens: an eastern Manchurian forest people who overthrew the Khitans, founded the Jin dynasty (1115–1234), and drove the Song dynasty out of north China in 1127; ancestors of the Manchus who took over China in the seventeenth century and ruled as the Qing dynasty until 1911

Jurkin: Borjigin sublineage; its leader, Sacha-beki, was Temüjin's first cousin

Juyongguan: pass (*guan*) in the mountains, which protected access to the north Chinese capital city at present-day Beijing

Kereyits: large and powerful tribal federation with a ruling clan inhabiting the Orkhon and Selenge River valleys in central Mongolia, practiced Nestorian Christianity, engaged in trade and relations with nomads and with settled peoples to the south (Tanguts, Jurchens, and central Asians)

keshig: Chinggis Khan's imperial guard, an elite organization at the center of Mongol power

khaghan: khan of khans or great khan, a title first assumed by Chinggis's third son and successor, Ögedei, a Turkic title adopted early into Mongolian; *also kaghan, qaghan, qa'an*

khatun: queen or princess, feminine partner (or daughter) of a khan; *also qatun*

Khitans: a Mongolic-speaking nomadic people who founded the Liao Empire (see Liao); *also Qitans*

khuda: relative by marriage and important ally

Khurasan: northern Persia, southwest of Transoxania in central Asia

khuriltai (Mo.): assembly of chieftains, princes, and commanders to confer on matters requiring collective decisions such as election of a new khan, initiation of a new campaign, and so on. Antecedent of today's Mongolian parliament, the Hural

Kiyat: another name for the ruling Mongol lineage (or sublineage) of the Borjigin

kut: Heaven's favor

levirate: a custom among nomadic peoples wherein (in the Mongol case) a deceased man's wife may be married to the man's younger brother or son by another woman, thus keeping the family together and providing for widows; not obligatory among upper-class Mongol women

Liao: empire and dynasty of the Khitans, 907–1125, originating in southwestern Manchuria (present-day eastern Inner Mongolia) and unifying large parts of north Asia (Mongolia, Manchuria, the northern fringe of China). The dynastic name of Liao was adopted by an ambitious chieftain in 947, after the river valley of their homeland.

The Khitans bequeathed to the Mongols the *ordo* system of tent-palaces and guards, and other administrative practices

mandate of Heaven (*tian ming*): ancient Chinese theory that an active, willing Heaven supported benevolent rulers but withheld its approval from despotic ones, justifying their replacement

Merkits: several tribal groupings (three), inhabiting forests south of Lake Baikal and northwest of the Mongols; not unified during most of the twelfth century

***mingghan*:** unit of one thousand men in an inner Asian military organization

myriarchy: (Mo.) *tümen*; a unit of ten thousand men in inner Asian military organization

Naimans: Turkicized tribal federation with a chiefly clan in western Mongolia, inhabiting northern and southern slopes of the Altai Mountains; influenced by the more advanced Uighur Turkic civilization in eastern central Asia; Nestorian, shamanistic

Nestorian Christianity: a "heretical" Christian sect taking its name from Nestorius (fifth century CE), patriarch of Constantinople, whose belief in the dual nature of Christ, human and divine, got him condemned; the sect spread into Persia and beyond, and still survives in Iraq today

***nökör*:** (plural *nököd*) companion, comrade-in-arms, non-kin follower

***noyan*:** commander (of a thousand), official, nobleman

Oirats: tribes west of Lake Baikal in the forest zone, not highly organized in twelfth century, played important role in later Mongolian history

Onggirats: small tribes pasturing northwest of the Önggüt in southern Mongolia, daughters commonly married Mongols, making them *khuda* (marriage partners) of the Golden Lineage

Önggüts: Turkic peoples inhabiting the steppes between north central China and Mongolia, northeastern neighbors of the Tanguts, enrolled as Jin frontier guards

***ordo*:** palace encampment (tent), from which derives the English word "horde"

Ordos: the arid steppe contained within the northern loop of the Yellow River in present-day Shaanxi Province and Inner Mongolia of the People's Republic of China

***otchigin*:** "hearth prince," youngest son, guardian of the parents' hearth

Qara Khitai: "black Khitai," the central Asian Empire founded by a scion of the Khitan imperial family after Liao fell to the Jurchens in 1124. Some Khitans fled out into central Asia and regrouped, others stayed behind and served (reluctantly) the new Jin dynasty. Conventionally dated 1131–1213 (1218); also *Qara-Qitai*, etc.

Qarluq: Turkic nomads of the central Asian steppes between the Tianshan range (in western China) and Lake Balkash; Muslims, moved southwest in the fifteenth and later centuries, some into northwest Afghanistan

Qayaliq: town in central Asia on lower Chu River (see Map 3)

Qipchaqs: Turkic tribes of the steppes from Kazakhstan to the southern Russian plains, not unified, the core nomadic population of the Golden Horde (see Desht-i Qipchaq); *also Kipchak*

***sechen*:** wise, prudent; a common Mongol epithet attached to names

Secret History: narrative epic with verse compiled in the mid-thirteenth century (date disputed) by inner members of the Mongol imperial clan, as a record of their origins and rise to power; contains evidence of later interpellations (tampering) by adherents of the Toluids who came to power with Khubilai; original Mongolian text was lost and has been reconstructed from surviving Chinese transcriptions and quotations in later Mongolian chronicles

Seljuks: Turkic dynasties in Anatolia and southwest Asia (southwest central Asia) from tenth century to early thirteenth century; the Mongol invasions spelled the end of Seljuk power and paved the way for the Osmanli or Ottomans to move into Anatolia

Sogdian: Iranian-speaking people who lived in the Ferghana valley (present-day Uzbekistan) and traveled the Silk Road in the early centuries CE as merchants and intermediaries between steppe nomads and settled societies; their script became the basis of the Uighur writing system that was borrowed by the Mongols

Tajik: Iranian-speaking Muslim of central Asia; Tajik language is indistinguishable from Persian

Tangut Xia: Tanguts, a Sino-Tibetan speaking people, founded Xia state, which controlled Hexi in northwest China, conventionally dated 1038–1227; *also Xi Xia, Tanggud* (Mo.)

Tatars: important and powerful tribe of southeast Mongolia, enemies of the twelfth-century Mongols, name became synonymous with the Mongol Empire in Russia and Europe; *also Tartar*

Tayichi'ut: a leading Mongol clan, relatives and rivals of the Kiyad–Borjigin to khanship, supported Jamukha, defeated by Chinggis Khan in 1201

Tengri: *tenggeri*, Mongolian word meaning "Heaven" or "sky" or sky-deity

tian ming: (Ch.) "Heaven's order" (see mandate of Heaven)

Transoxania: the region of southern central Asia between the Amu Darya and Syr Darya (rivers), which flow into the Aral Sea

tümen: a myriarchy, or division of ten thousand soldiers, in inner Asian military practice

Turkestan: another term for central Asia; thus eastern Turkestan refers to Chinese central Asia (present-day Xinjiang) and western Turkestan to Transoxania, Khwarazm, and the steppes north of them (present-day republics of central Asia)

Uighurs: Turkic peoples in eastern central Asia (today's Chinese Xinjiang Uighur Autonomous Region, although the latter Uighurs are not directly descended from those of the twelfth century), who by late twelfth century had mostly settled into oasis towns as merchants and farmers, were literate, Nestorian or Buddhist, and politically sophisticated; *also Uygur, Uyghur, etc.*

ulus: joint patrimony of Mongol nobles; also, the lands that evolved into independent khanates (territory ruled by a khan) under the elder sons of Chinggis Khan and their descendants

Yasakh: Chinggis Khan's reputed code of laws or important precedents, concerning mainly the military, hunt, and postal system; its nature remains subject of scholarly debate

Yuan: Chinese dynasty formally founded by Khubilai Khan, conventionally dated 1271–1368; the term often refers to the entire period beginning with enthronement of Chinggis Khan in 1206, or with the accession to power of Khubilai in 1260

References

A list of selected general and specialized sources follows the chapter citations. For a general reader, aside from the more popular accounts by Jack Weatherford and British travel writer-historian John Man, the single best and most accessible scholarly treatment of the Mongol Empire remains David Morgan's recently updated *The Mongols*. A concise new book by Israeli scholar Michal Biran, *Chinggis Khan* (2007) explores in detail the place of the conqueror and his changing image in Islamic history and historiography.

Readers with a particular interest in military history should turn to Timothy May's *The Mongol Art of War* (2007). These two books reached the author too late to be consulted in depth, but their general premises are shared with those of this book.

Chapter References

Quoted passages in each chapter, beginning with the quotation under chapter titles, are identified by author, edition, or date of publication of the source, and page or paragraph number. Full information about the source can be found in the list of the most important works consulted for this biography that follows, arranged alphabetically by the author's or translator's last name. The works of other authors mentioned are also listed by chapter; some specific sources consulted for Chapter 10 appear in the references for that chapter, though these works do not exhaust the literature drawn upon for that or any other chapter.

Introduction: Adshead 1993, 53; Abu-Lughod 1989, 182; Juvaini 1997, 4; on Sun Yat-sen's reference to Chinese Muslims as "Tartars" see Tuttle 2005, 66.

One: Mongol proverb quoted from Jagchid and Hyer 1979, 22; Bentley 1993, 111; Di Cosmo 1999; Bentley 1996; Christian 1994;Gibbon 1914, 1; Allsen 2001; Barfield 1993; Golden 2003; Fletcher 1986; Khazanov 1984, 82 for the quotation from Mahmud Kashgari; Allsen, *Culture and Conquest*, 11 *passim*; Lindner 1982, 701, 710; Di Cosmo 1999, 13, 23, *passim*; Allsen 2006; Golden 2003; Biran 2005 on the Liao Khitans and Khara Khitai.

Two: Secret History para. 1 in de Rachewiltz 2004, I; de Rachewiltz 2004 I, 234; Allsen 1997b, 4; Juvaini in Boyle, I, 21–22.

Three: Secret History paras. 76, 75, 76, 78, 89, 93, 96, 103; for historians' speculations on Father Mönglik's marriage to Hö'elün, see de Rachewiltz 2004, vol. 1, 339.

Four: Secret History paras. 126, 108, 110, 254, 117, 127, 126, 134; for the Chinese diplomat's account, *Mengda beilu*, see Atwood, "A Complete Record of the Mong Tatars."

Five: Secret History paras. 196, 143, 145, 149, 148, 153, 154; Marco Polo (Yule-Cordier edn), vol. 1, 239; *Yuan Shi* ch. 120, 9; on Baljuna see Cleaves 1955 and Atwood 2004; *Secret History* paras. 189, 196, 201, 208; Rashid al-Din (*Sbornik letopisei*, 1952, 119; Thackston, 1998, 181).

Six: Secret History para. 216; de Rachewiltz 2004, vol. 1, 460; Allsen 2006, 135; Dawson/Carpini, *Mission to Asia*, 14–15; *Secret History* paras. 203, 246; Jackson 2005, 258, on evolving Mongol religion; Dawson/ Carpini, 9; DiCosmo 1999 on factors contributing to expansion of steppe empires.

Seven: Secret History para. 249; Juvaini, 68, 78–81; *Secret History* para. 254–255.

Eight: Juvaini, 99, 103–104, 134; Waley/*Travels*, 116, 93, 97, 103; Juvaini, 105, 107.

Nine: Rashid al-Din (Thackston 1998), 262; *Secret History* paras. 256, 268; Atwood 2004, 349; Bold 2000; Biran 2007 ch. 5 on Chinggis's changing image in Muslim eyes; Rashid al-Din's evaluation of Chinggis Khan (Thackston 1998),144; Juvaini's assessment of Chinggis Khan, 24–26; Atwood 2005; Juvaini, 129; Rashid al-Din, 293–297.

Ten: Gibbon, vol. 7, 1; Biran, ch. 5; Guyug's letter of 1246 to Pope Innocent IV in Dawson/*Mission to Asia*, 85–86; Tatiana Zerjal, et al., 717–721; Sun Laichen; Allsen, "Ever closer encounters," *Commodity and exchange in the Mongol empire* and "Robing in the Mongolian Empire;" Marco Polo, vol. 1, p. 387; Allsen, "Mongolian Princes and their merchant partners, 1200–1260; Allsen, *Culture and Conquest in Mongol Eurasia*; Birge 1995; Ostrowski, ch. 1, *passim*; Halperin 2002; McChesney 1996, 121–141.

Sources

Abu-Lughod, Janet L. 1989. *Before European Hegemony: The World System A.D. 1250–1350*. New York: Oxford University Press.

Adshead, S. A. M. 1993. *Central Asia in World History*. New York: St. Martin's Press.

Allsen, Thomas T. 1994. "The rise of Mongolian empire and Mongolian rule in north China," in Herbert Franke and Denis Twitchett, eds. *The Cambridge History of China Volume 6: Alien Regimes and Border States, 907–1368*. Cambridge, MA: Cambridge University Press, 321–365.

———. 1987. *Mongol Imperialism. The Policies of the Grand Qan Mögke in China, Russia, and the Islamic Lands, 1251–1259*. Berkeley, CA: University of California Press.

———. 1989. "Mongolian princes and their merchant partners, 1200–1260." *Asia Major* 3rd series, Vol. 2, no. 2, 83–126.

———. 1997a. *Commodity and Exchange in the Mongol Empire. A Cultural History of Islamic Textiles*. Cambridge, MA: Cambridge University Press.

———. 1997b. "Ever closer encounters: The appropriation of cultures and the apportionment of peoples in the Mongol Empire." *Journal of Early Modern History*, Vol. 1, 2–23.

———. 2001. *Culture and Conquest in Mongol Eurasia*. Cambridge, MA: Cambridge University Press, 2001.

———. 2001. "Sharing out the empire: Apportioned lands under the Mongols." In Anatoly M. Khazanov and André Wink, eds. *Nomads in the Sedentary World*. Richmond, Surrey: Curzon, 172–190.

———. 2001. "Robing in the Mongolian Empire." In Steward Gorden, ed. *Robes and Honor: The Medieval World of Investiture*. New York: Palgrave, 305–313.

———. 2002. "Mongol imperial government after Činggis Qan." In Wendy F. Kasinec and Michael A. Polushin, eds. *Expanding Empires. Cultural Interaction and Exchange in World Societies from Ancient to Early Modern Times*. The World Beat Series, No. 2. Wilmington, DE: Scholarly Resources, 177–185.

———. 2006. "Technologies of governance in the Mongolian Empire: A geographic overview." In David Sneath, ed. *Imperial Statecraft: Political Forms and Techniques of Governance in Inner Asia, Sixth-Twentieth Centuries*. Bellingham, WA: Center for East Asian Studies, Western Washington University, 117–140.

Amitai, Reuven and Michal Biran, ed. 2005. *Mongols, Turks, and Others*. Leiden and Boston: Brill.

Anon. *The Secret History of the Mongols*. See under Igor deRachewiltz. An abridged adaptation from the translation published in 1983 by F. W. Cleaves was done by Paul Kahn, *The Secret History of the Mongols, The Origins of Chingis Khan*. Rpt. Boston: Cheng & Tsui, 1998.

Atwood, Christopher .P. 2004. *Encyclopedia of Mongolia and the Mongol Empire*. New York: Facts on File, Inc.

———. 2005. "A complete record of the Mong Tatars" by Zhao Gong of the Song. Unpublished translation of the *Mengda beilu*. A German translation by Erich Haenisch and Yao Ts'ung-wu was edited and published by Peter Olbricht and Elisabeth Pinks, *Meng-Ta pei-lu und Hei-Ta shih-lüeh* (Wiesbaden: Otto Harrassowitz, 1980). Most scholars read the envoy's name as Zhao Hong.

Barfield, Thomas. 2001. "Steppe empires, China and the Silk Route: Nomads as a force in international trade and politics." In Anatoly M. Khazanov and André Wink, eds. *Nomads in the Sedentary World*. Richmond, Surrey: Curzon, 234–249.

Bartlett, Robert. 1993. *The Making of Europe: Conquest, Colonization and Cultural Change, 950–1350*. Princeton, N.J.: Princeton University Press.

Bentley, Jerry H. 1993. *Old World Encounters: Cross-Cultural Contacts and Exchanges in Pre-Modern Times*. New York and Oxford: Oxford University Press.

———. 1996. "Cross-cultural interaction and periodization in world history." *American Historical Review*, Vol. 101 (June), 749–770.

Biran, Michal. 2005. *The Empire of the Qara Khitai in Eurasian History; Between China and the Islamic World*. Cambridge, England: Cambridge University Press.

———. 2007. *Chinggis Khan*. In the series *Makers of the Muslim World*. Oxford, England: Oneworld Publications.

Birge, Bettine. 1995. "Levirate marriage and the revival of widow chastity in Yüan China." *Asia Major* 3rd series, Vol. 8, no. 2, 107–146.

Bold, Bat-Ochir. 2000. "The death and burial of Chinggis Khaan." *Central Asian Survey*, Vol. 19, no. 1, 95–115.

Buell, Paul. 1999. "Mongol Empire and Turkicization: The evidence of food and foodways." In Reuven Amitai-Preiss and David O. Morgan, eds. *The Mongol Empire and Its Legacy*. Leiden: Brill, 200–223.

Christian, David. 1994. "Inner Eurasia as a unit of world history." *Journal of World History*, Vol. 5, no. 2, 173–211.

Cleaves, Francis W. 1995. "The historicity of the Baljuna covenant." *Harvard Journal of Asiatic Studies*, Vol. 18, 357–421.

Dawson, Christopher. 1980. *Mission to Asia*. Toronto: University of Toronto Press; translation of accounts by John of Plano Carpini, William of Rubruck, and other 13th-century travelers. For a new translation and edition of William of Rubruck, see under Peter Jackson.

Di Cosmo, Nicola. 1999. "State formation and periodization in inner Asian history." *Journal of World History*, Vol. 10, no. 1, 1–40.

Dunnell, Ruth. 1991. "The fall of the Xia Empire: Sino-steppe relations in the late 12th–early 13th centuries." In Gary Seaman and Daniel Marks, eds. *Rulers from the Steppe: State Formation on the Eurasian Periphery.* Los Angeles, CA: Ethnographic Press, Center for Visual Anthropology, University of Southern California, 158–185.

Fletcher, Joseph. 1986. "The Mongols: Ecological and social perspectives." *Harvard Journal of Asiatic Studies*, Vol. 46, no. 1, 11–50.

Gibbon, Edward. 1914. *The Decline and Fall of the Roman Empire.* 7 vols. ed. By J. B. Bury. London: Methuen & Co., Ltd. Volume 7, ch. LXIV.

Golden, Peter. 1992. *An Introduction to the History of the Turkic Peoples.* Wiesbaden: Otto Harrassowitz.

———. 2003. *Nomads and Sedentary Societies in Medieval Eurasia.* In the series *Essays on Global and Comparative History.* Washington, D.C.: American Historical Association.

Haining, Thomas N. 1999. "The vicissitudes of Mongolian historiography in the twentieth century." In Reuven Amitai-Preiss and David O. Morgan, eds. *The Mongol Empire and Its Legacy.* Leiden: Brill, 332–346.

Halperin, Charles J. 1985. *Russian and the Golden Horde: The Mongol Impact on Medieval Russian History.* Bloomington, IN: Indiana University Press.

———. 2002. "Russia and the Mongols." In Wendy F. Kasinec and Michael A. Polushin, eds. *Expanding Empires. Cultural Interaction and Exchange in World Societies from Ancient to Early Modern Times.* The World Beat Series, No. 2. Wilmington, DE: Scholarly Resources, 197–207.

de Hartog, Leo. 1989. *Genghis Khan, Conqueror of the World.* New York: St. Martin's Press.

Jackson, Peter. 1999. "From Ulus to Khanate: The making of the Mongols states, c. 1220–c. 1290." In Reuven Amitai-Preiss and David O. Morgan, eds. *The Mongol Empire and Its Legacy.* Leiden: Brill, 12–37.

———, transl. 1990. *The Mission of Friar William of Rubruck. His Journey to the Court of the Great Khan Möngke, 1253–1255.* London: The Hakkluyt Society.

———. 2005. "The Mongols and the faith of the conquered." In Reuven Amitai and Michal Biran, eds. *Mongols, Turks, and Others*, 245–290. Leiden and Boston: Brill.

Jagchid, Sechen and Paul Hyer. 1979. *Mongolia's Culture and Society.* Boulder, CO: Westview Press.

Juvaini, 'Ata Malik (13th c.). 1997. *Genghis Khan. The History of the World-Conqueror.* Transl. J. A. Boyle. 1958; rpt. Seattle, WA: University of Washington Press.

Khazanov, Anatoly M. 1984. *Nomads and the Outside World.* Cambridge, MA: Cambridge University Press.

Khazanov, Anatoly M. and André Wink, eds. 2001. *Nomads in the Sedentary World.* Richmond, Surrey: Curzon Press.

Lane, George. 2004. *Genghis Khan and Mongol Rule.* Westport, CT: Greenwood Press.

———. 2006. *Daily Life in the Mongol Empire.* Westport, CT: Greenwood Press.

Lindner, Rudi Paul. 1982. "What was a nomadic tribe?" *Society for the Comparative Study of History and Society*, Vol. 24, no. 4, 689–711.

Man, John. 2004. *Genghis Khan. Life, Death and Resurrection.* London and New York: Bantam Press.

Manz, Beatrice. 1989. *Rise and Rule of Tamerlane.* Cambridge, MA: Cambridge University Press.

Marco Polo. 1993. *The Travels of Marco Polo. The Complete Yule-Cordier Edition.* 2 Vols. New York: Dover Publications.

May, Timothy. 2007. *The Mongol Art of War.* Chicago, IL: Westholme Publications.

McChesney, R. D. 1996. *Central Asia: Foundations of Change.* Princeton, NJ: Darwin Press.

Morgan, David. 2007. *The Mongols.* New York, NY: Basil Blackwell, 2nd edn.

Ostrowski, Donald. 1998. *Muscovy and the Mongols.* Cambridge, MA: Cambridge University Press.

de Rachewiltz, Igor. 2004. *The Secret History of the Mongols. A Mongolian Epic of the Thirteenth Century.* Two Volumes. Leiden and Boston: Brill.

———, et al., eds. 1993. *In the Service of the Khan. Eminent Personalities of the Early Mongol-Yüan Period.* Wiesbaden: Harrassowitz Verlag.

Rashid al-Din (14th c.). 1998. *Jami'u't-tawarikh (Compendium of Chronicles).* Transl. W. M. Thackston. (Limited publication of the *Sources of Oriental Languages and Literature Series* at Harvard University). Russian transl by O. I. Smirnova, *Rashid al-Din, Sbornik Letopisei, Vol. 1, book 2.* Moscow and Leningrad: Izdatel'stvo Akademii Nauk, 1952.

Ratchnevsky, Paul. 1991. *Genghis Khan, His Life and Legacy.* Trans. Thomas Nivison Haining. Oxford: Basil Blackwell.

Subtelny, Maria Eva. 1994. "The symbiosis of Turk and Tajik." In Beatrice F. Manz, ed. *Central Asia in Historical Perspective.* Boulder, CO: Westview Press, 45–61.

Sun, Laichen. 2006. "Gemstone trade in Asia, 1279–1911." Paper presented at the annual meeting of the Association for Asian Studies, San Francisco, CA 6–9 April 2006.

Sung, Lian., et al. 1976. *Yuan Shih (Dynastic History of the Yuan).* Po-na edn. Beijing: Zhonghua shuju.

Tuttle, Gray. 2005. *Tibetan Buddhists in the Making of Modern China.* New York: Columbia University Press.

Waley, Arthur. 1978. *The Travels of an Alchemist.* London, 1931; rpt. Taipei: Southern Materials Center; translation of the diary kept by Daoist master Changchun's traveling companion.

Weatherford, Jack. 2004. *Genghis Khan and the Making of the Modern World.* New York: Crown Publications.

Zerjal, Tatiana. et al. 2003. "The genetic legacy of the Mongols." *American Journal of Human Genetics*, Vol. 72, 717–721.

Index